RABINDRANATH TAGORE

Professor Debarati Bandyopadhyay teaches at the Department of English, Visva-Bharati, Santiniketan. She was a Post-Doctoral Fellow for two years (2010–11) at Rabindranath Tagore Centre for Human Development Studies, Kolkata. She was an International Visiting Fellow at the University of Essex in 2017, and in 2018, a Visiting Fellow and Scholar at Glasgow and the Scottish Centre of Tagore Studies in Edinburgh, respectively, to conduct research on new nature writing and ecocriticism. Nature and Tagore are the biggest influences in her life.

RABINDRANATH TAGORE

~ A Life of Intimacy with Nature ~

Debarati Bandyopadhyay

Published by
Rupa Publications India Pvt. Ltd 2019
7/16, Ansari Road, Daryaganj
New Delhi 110002

Sales centres:
Allahabad Bengaluru Chennai
Hyderabad Jaipur Kathmandu
Kolkata Mumbai

Copyright © Debarati Bandyopadhyay 2019

The views and opinions expressed in this book are the
author's own and the facts are as reported by him/her which
have been verified to the extent possible, and the publishers
are not in any way liable for the same.

All rights reserved.
No part of this publication may be reproduced, transmitted, or
stored in a retrieval system, in any form or by any means, electronic,
mechanical, photocopying, recording or otherwise, without the prior
permission of the publisher.

ISBN: 978-93-5333-456-7

First impression 2019

10 9 8 7 6 5 4 3 2 1

The moral right of the author has been asserted.

Printed at Nutech Print Services, Faridabad

This book is sold subject to the condition that it shall not, by way of
trade or otherwise, be lent, resold, hired out, or otherwise circulated,
without the publisher's prior consent, in any form of binding or cover
other than that in which it is published.

Contents

Preface — *vii*

Introduction — *xxv*

1. The Storm: *Glimpses of Bengal* and *Gora* — 1
2. The Calm: Ecophilosophy in *Gitanjali* and Beyond — 48
3. Eco-ethics: *The Waterfall* (*Muktadhara*) and *Red Oleanders* (*Raktakarabi*) — 86
4. In Search of Lost Harmony: Nature and Modernity in Rabindranath's Works — 121
5. Environmental Activism: Santiniketan-Sriniketan — 154

Conclusion — 177

Acknowledgements — 189

Bibliography — 191

Preface

Rabindranath Tagore (1861–1941) is famous in literary and artistic circles as the first and, so far, sole Indian recipient of the Nobel Prize in Literature, which he received in 1913 for *Gitanjali: Song Offerings* (1912). He wrote the national anthems of India and Bangladesh, and arguably inspired that of Sri Lanka as well. But we cannot understand the life and work of Tagore by only highlighting these achievements. A section of Indians revere him as the founder of Visva-Bharati in Santiniketan, 'the abode of peace'. This institution became a central university, according to an Act of the Indian Parliament in 1951—ten years after its creator had left for his eternal abode of peace. His enormous literary, musical and artistic output is still undergoing the process of evaluation and appreciation in different countries. Tagore scholars continue to unearth new facets of his life and work even in the twenty-first century. Among the traditional fields of Tagore studies, some critics focus on his portrayal of the changing moods of nature, scenes of human vulnerability and fortitude, national and international politics and, through all the suffering, a profound faith reposed in God.

Thousands of pages have been written in both Bengali and English, in appreciation of Rabindranath Tagore's writings on nature. The greater part of this critical work has been devoted to the analyses of the felicity of expression of natural beauty in his writings. Lately though, some works in Bengali and English have concentrated on the presentation of environment in his writings, and the buildings of Santiniketan that he had commissioned.[1] This aspect of his work needs better representation, especially in view of the current global environmental crisis. It is necessary, for our own welfare, to understand Rabindranath's contribution to this field as a writer and activist.

Pollution is not merely a problem; it is the most prominent index to the global malaise that started with the process of industrialization. Many things affect our physical surroundings or the environment, and human activities are not the least of these. We also need to pay attention to the dynamic relationship between the air, water and soil of a place, and the human and nonhuman life there—the concept of ecology. Human beings have proved themselves to be rather selfish creatures. We pay attention to certain issues regarding the environment and ecology only when our own survival as a species is threatened. And even then, issues related to the survival of other living beings and the planet itself remain matters of secondary importance.

Still, so long as this selfish anthropocentric desire

for survival prompts us to pay attention to the flora and fauna of a place, the result benefits not only that particular place, but the entire world. Environmental activists, in the last few decades, have variously attempted to petition, prompt, lobby, demand, agitate and even turn violent to compel governments to adopt green measures that ensure our survival and sustenance. In the USA, in 1962, for instance, the publication of Rachel Carson's *Silent Spring* alerted the government to the fact of an indiscriminate use of chemical pesticides and herbicides produced by multinational companies. As a result of this, Carson was reviled by many groups with vested economic and political interests. Ultimately, the US government had to introduce measures to safeguard the lives of the citizens against these potentially fatal chemicals. Though some multinational companies continued to sell DDT and similar chemical products in underdeveloped countries, Rachel Carson's lone vigil continues to be saluted by environmental activists and ecocritics everywhere even today.

In the academic world, since the 1970s, ecocriticism[2] has established itself as an essential field of critical studies. Ecocriticism is usually described as the critical study of the various levels of the relationship between literature and the environment. This often turns out to be an exciting intellectual position, as one can critically estimate William Shakespeare's presentation of the island in *The Tempest*; concentrate on William Wordsworth's reverence for nature in England; or discuss Henry David Thoreau's attachment to

Walden in the USA. One may also critique Charles Dickens and Elizabeth Gaskell's writings from the mid-1850s, about the deteriorating environment of the factory towns in the north of England, which represented the darker side of the Industrial Revolution. One can discuss the literary stance against the use of nuclear, chemical and biological weapons, and analyse the relevance of works of science and speculative fiction that imagine the contemporary world on the brink of destruction, as in the writings of the Canadian author Margaret Atwood. The sheer range of the possible literary approaches to nature and the 'environment' question represents, therefore, expressions of human emotions spanning the sedate on one end and the angry on the other, with subtle nuances of the ironical existing somewhere in the middle. Ecocriticism is a fairly comprehensive term today as literary critics with leanings towards environmentalism, deep ecology, eco-socialism, ecofeminism and postcolonial ecocriticism contribute to it in their own ways.

This critical process started in the USA in the second half of the twentieth century and later spread to England and Europe. Countries like India joined the ecocritical debate much later, in the fairly recent decades. It is necessary, in this context, to differentiate between the literary texts that have existed since the last decades of the eighteenth century as powerful criticism of the pollution that came in with the Industrial Revolution, and the critical field of ecocriticism that emerged almost 200 years later. Hence, when we say that

Indians became aware of the subtle ecocritical arguments recently, we are not taking into account the existence of possible literary critiques of the environment and the ecological conditions in the past in India.

Rabindranath Tagore has not generally been considered in ecocritical circles as relevant to the current environmental debate so far. Therefore, in this volume, an attempt has been made to show how an ecocritical evaluation of Tagore today can make us acknowledge him as a pioneering thinker and activist in this area. He worked tirelessly throughout his life for the sustenance of ecological harmony. In order to appreciate this, it is necessary to read his life and work in terms of an ecobiography.

There are autobiographical anecdotes in Tagore's *Jibansmriti* and *Chhelebela*, as well as his numerous Bengali and English essays, lectures and letters. Prabhat Kumar Mukhopadhyay's four-volume *Rabindrajibani* and Prashanta Kumar Pal's multivolume *Rabijibani* are monumental works in Bengali that remain unsurpassed. There is also Krishna Kripalani's *Rabindranath Tagore: A Biography* and Uma Dasgupta's biography of Tagore as well as *My Life in My Words*. As Tagore scholars may express dismay at the thought of an attempt at writing Tagore's biography afresh, a disclaimer would be in order at the outset: an ecobiography is not an attempt at writing an account of all the activities of a renowned person.

Tagore's biographical details are voluminous, but it is possible to present a bare outline of his life in a few paragraphs. He was born on 7 May 1861 (25 Baisakh 1268 in the Bengali calendar) as the fourteenth child to Maharshi Debendranath Tagore and Sarada Devi in the sprawling and teeming family mansion at Jorasanko in Calcutta (now known as Kolkata), just four years after the Sepoy Mutiny of 1857, which had resulted in the British Crown taking over the power to govern India from the East India Company. Calcutta was then the capital of India. In Calcutta, Debendranath Tagore, the son of Prince Dwarkanath Tagore, and a disciple of Raja Ram Mohan Roy, was the leader of the Brahmo Samaj, which refused to worship the proverbial 33 crore Hindu idols and reposed faith in one God, following the Upanishads. The family had land and other property and was rich, though with many members and dependents. It was one of the pioneers in initiating and sustaining the Bengal Renaissance. In his childhood, young Rabi was often confined to a room within the house, with servants taking care of him as he continued to yearn for the world outside. A series of tutors taught him different subjects at home. He attended schools, but only for brief periods as he did not like the formal atmosphere of the classroom and the rigidity of the teaching process. In 1873, the investiture of the sacred thread took place and young Rabi was deeply influenced by his father's enunciation of the gayatri mantra taught during the ceremony. He accompanied his father to Bolpur (Santiniketan), Amritsar and Dalhousie soon after and received important lessons in the Vedas, Upanishads, ancient Sanskrit texts, history, geography, English, mathematics and astronomy during this period. In his adolescence, he was first trained by his brother Satyendranath in Ahmedabad, and then in Bombay (now Mumbai) by the family of Dr Turkhud, in British culture and etiquette. At the age of seventeen, in 1878, he was sent to Brighton, where he was accommodated by Jnanadanandini Devi, Satyendranath's wife, who was bringing up her young children, Surendranath and Indira, there. Later, he went to University College London for his law studies but returned to India in March 1880 with Satyendranath's family, without completing the course, presumably on his father's orders. In 1881, his proposed second voyage to England was aborted in Madras (now Chennai) on the request of his travel companion.

On his return, he stayed with his elder brother Jyotirindranath, the talented dramatist, and his wife Kadambari Devi. The latter was nearly Rabindranath's age, but still became his guardian after the death of his mother on 11 March 1875. They lived in a riverside villa at Chandernagore. Rabindranath loved the Ganges, the banks of which had not been cluttered with factories at that time. In 1882, the trio was living in a rented house on Sudder Street, near the Museum in Calcutta. Here, one day, Rabindranath was gazing at the sunrise through the leaves of the trees in the neighbourhood, when he suddenly felt as if a cover had been lifted from his eyes and there was a great radiance bathing the world. He felt this for three days. The result was a long poem, 'Nirjharer Swapnabhanga' (The Awakening of the Waterfall), a testament to his ability to spiritually feel at one with even the most trivial things and creatures in existence.

In Jorasanko, Kadambari Devi used to host the foremost literary figures in Calcutta and these sessions enriched Rabindranath. In 1883, he was married to the ten-year-old Mrinalini Devi. In April 1884, tragedy struck with the untimely death of his first literary critic and caring sister-in-law, Kadambari Devi. He continued to cherish the memory of her literary sessions and unstinted help for the rest of his life. He also wrote in the family monthlies, *Bharati* and *Balak*, at the time. The Maharshi made Rabindranath the secretary of the Brahmo Samaj, for which he composed beautiful hymns.

The formal foundation of the Santiniketan Ashram took place on 19 October 1888. In 1889, Rabindranath, now the father of Madhurilata (or Bela) and Rathindranath, went to Sholapur with his family. He visited his beloved Ghazipur too. In August 1890, he started for his second stint in England, but there are signs of him missing his family in *Europe Jatrir Diary*. On his return to Calcutta in November 1890, *Manasi* was published and he became famous as a Bengali poet. Soon, Rabindranath was sent to supervise the vast family estate in places now belonging primarily to Bangladesh. He had a growing family in Calcutta, which the estate took care of. His family later came to live with him in an outlying district.

He soon found it difficult to continue to play host to a steady stream of friends and British officials visiting the family, as they made demands on the time he wanted to devote to his writings. During this period, he received a monthly stipend amounting to ₹260, which was later increased to ₹300, considered to be a modest sum in terms of the family's social standing. It was barely adequate for the family living in the districts. Rabindranath tried to work towards agriculture-based enterprises and took loans for the purpose. Through these activities, he wanted to help the rural people. He had limited financial means but unlimited opportunities to experience the river Padma from the large family boat (also called Padma), and write letters, poems and short stories. The people that he met during this period populate, in various guises, the stories of *Galpaguchha*. The period between 1891 and 1895 is called the 'Sadhana' period of his life, named so after the magazine to which he was a prolific contributor. He also wrote the *Chhinnapatra* letters, primarily to his niece, Indira Devi, during this period.

In 1901, Rabindranath got his daughters, Madhurilata and Renuka, married off in June and August respectively, with Maharshi Debendranath bearing the expenses. He moved to Santiniketan with Mrinalini Devi and the other three children, with his father's blessings. He started the innovative residential Brahmacharyashram school on 22 December 1901 (7 Poush 1308 in the Bengali calendar) with five students, his eldest son Rathindranath being one of them. Mrinalini Devi was generous in showering her affection and belongings on the school, where the students did not have to pay for tuition, board and lodging. The school started expanding.

Rabindranath lost his wife Mrinalini Devi on 23 November 1902 and daughter Renuka on 14 September 1903. He immersed himself in the affairs of the school and his writings. On 19 January 1905, he lost his father, and in 1907, his youngest son, Samindranath. During these initial years of the school and throughout the rest of his life, Rabindranath had to move from place to place in India and abroad in order to make people aware of his distinctive vision regarding education and to get money for Visva-Bharati by delivering lectures, selling the rights to his books and approaching possible patrons who would take care of some aspect of the institutional necessities.

His novel *Gora* was published in 1910. In 1911, Rabindranath finished writing *Jibansmriti*, the memoir. In 1912, he took to London a manuscript containing the English translations of his Bengali poems from *Gitanjali* and a few other volumes of poetry. In London, W.B. Yeats, Ezra Pound and the artist William Rothenstein appreciated the poems and these were published by the India Society of London in 1912, as *Gitanjali: Song Offerings*, with Yeats writing the introduction. Rabindranath travelled to the USA in 1912, visited Rathindranath, who was a student of agricultural science in Illinois, and delivered a series of lectures in 1913, in Urbana, Chicago, Boston and Wisconsin. He returned to London in April 1913 and delivered lectures and read from his plays in London and Oxford. It was during this time that Thomas Sturge Moore, an English poet, proposed his name for the Nobel Prize.

Rabindranath soon returned to India, and learned on 16 November 1913, while he was residing in Santiniketan, that he had been awarded the Nobel Prize for Literature. He received the Nobel Prize diploma, medal and a cheque for ₹1,16,269 from Lord Carmichael in the Governor House in Calcutta on 29 January 1914, of which ₹48,000 was deposited at the Patisar agricultural bank and ₹27,000 at the Kaligram agricultural bank. The interest received from the deposit was spent on the school in Santiniketan.

In November 1914, the students of the Phoenix Settlement of Mohandas Karamchand Gandhi in South Africa, visited Santiniketan. In 1915, Gandhi visited Rabindranath's school twice, in February and March, and inspired the students to do their own work. Visva-Bharati continues to commemorate this visit every year by celebrating a day of cleaning in which all the staff and students participate, on 10 March as 'Gandhi Punyaha'.

In 1915, Rabindranath was awarded a Knighthood but in 1919, as a mark of protest against the massacre of innocent men, women and children at Jallianwala Bagh, he wrote a passionate letter to Viceroy Chelmsford, renouncing it. In the meantime, in 1916–17, Sir Rabindranath visited Japan and the USA, speaking of nationalism and internationalism. On 23 December 1918, the foundation of Visva-Bharati was laid in Santiniketan. In 1916, *Ghare Baire* (*Home and the*

World) was published, generating serious debate about the protagonist Nikhil's refusal to boycott British goods.

Rabindranath delivered lectures in Bombay and Gujarat during this time. In May 1920, he started on a journey to Europe to disseminate knowledge about Visva-Bharati and gain support for the institution. Cities like London, Cambridge, Bristol, Paris and countries like the Netherlands, Belgium, and the USA were on his travel itinerary. In 1921, he retraced the route, delivering lectures in Boston, Chicago and Texas, after which he came to England, and then moved on to France, Switzerland, Denmark, Sweden, Germany, Austria, and Czechoslovakia, before returning to India. This was the time when he critiqued Gandhiji's cult of the charka and the Non-cooperation movement. On a positive note, Leonard Knight Elmhirst brought his expertise in agricultural matters, and Rabindranath initiated, with his help, the rural reconstruction work in Sriniketan, 'the abode of welfare' and Santiniketan's 'sibling', by adopting extremely backward villages in the vicinity of Surul. In 1922, he wrote *Muktadhara*, a play about State coercion, the battle between an aggressively mechanical civilization and the vulnerabilities of nature, and the margins of human society.

Rabindranath visited Ceylon (now known as Sri Lanka) in 1922. His discussions about rural reconstruction in villages near Santiniketan took place with Patrick and Arthur Geddes during this period. In 1923, Lord Lytton visited Santiniketan and Sriniketan, and the Surul rural reconstruction project received the government's help.

Rabindranath spent a lot of energy preparing eleven drafts of a play, which was ultimately titled *Raktakarabi* (*Red Oleanders*), about a mining town and the incursion of Nandini, a young girl, into this soul-killing space.

In 1924, his correspondence with Patrick Geddes continued. He visited China, Japan and France, and had to stop in Argentina on his way to Peru, due to an illness. Victoria Ocampo, a writer, hosted him in Argentina, taking good care of the ailing poet. His doodles started getting transformed into paintings. In 1925, he returned to India, travelling through Spain and Italy. His travels through Italy and his meeting with Benito Mussolini were decried by Romain Rolland in Switzerland in 1926. During this time, he also visited Elmhirst at Dartington Hall. Rabindranath's ideas regarding Santiniketan and Sriniketan had contributed to its making. He met Bertrand Russell, with whom he had been in correspondence for a number of years. In 1926, he travelled through Norway, Denmark, Germany, Austria, Hungary, Yugoslavia and Egypt. He visited Java and Bali in 1927, and Ceylon again in 1928, when, due to an illness, he could not travel to Oxford to deliver the Hibbert lectures.

1928 was an important year for Santiniketan and Sriniketan as Rabindranath conceptualized and implemented a unique way of celebrating nature on 14 July with the 'Briksharopan' ceremony, where representatives of the five elements brought saplings, which were then planted with great care; the short story 'Balai' was written by Rabindranath for the occasion. The monsoons, essential for agriculture, were also greeted during the celebration of 'Barshamangal', in Santiniketan. The next day, he instituted the 'Halakarshana', or the symbolical tilling of land, in Sriniketan.

In 1929, on reaching the USA from Japan, he lost his passport and the humiliating treatment by immigration officials prompted him to leave the country immediately. In 1930, he was finally able to deliver the Hibbert Lecture, on 'The Religion of Man,' to great critical acclaim in Oxford. His paintings were displayed at a Parisian Gallery courtesy of Victoria Ocampo and the French critics freely praised his work. The National Gallery in Berlin also wanted to buy some of his paintings. He met Einstein for the first time on 14 July 1930. He returned to India after visiting Denmark, Russia, Germany, the USA and England.

In 1931, *Gitabitan* was published with 1,500 songs written by him. In 1932, he undertook a memorable flight to Persia (now known as Iran). He visited Ceylon for the third time in 1934. The beginning of World War II in 1939 agitated the poet and he expressed dismay at the thought that his faith in Western civilization was possibly misplaced. On 19 February 1940, he asked Gandhiji to assume charge of Visva-Bharati after his death. He fell very ill in Kalimpong, in the northern part of Bengal, in September 1940. The poems from 'Arogya' (1940) and 'Janmadine' (1941) exist as testaments to his love for an Upanishadic harmony in life and beyond death. On 14 April 1941, 'Sabhyatar Sankat' was one of his last expressions denouncing war and aggression and it remains a desperate attempt to retain faith in humanity. He fell fatally ill in July and in spite of an operation conducted on him at his Jorasanko residence in Calcutta, passed away on 7 August 1941 (22 Shravan 1348 in the Bengali Calendar), thereby completing the circuit of his life, which started eighty years ago in the same mansion.

∞

In view of Rabindranath's travel to so many countries and his relentless efforts, first for the school and later for Visva-Bharati, it is a wonder that he wrote daily, composing more than 2,000 songs and writing thought-provoking novels. A world-famous poet, he was also a playwright, who consistently produced vignettes of his life through short stories, remained an indefatigable essayist and letter-writer in Bengali and English, delivered lectures in so many countries, and having taken up painting at the age of sixty, was on display in prestigious Western galleries too. In Visva-Bharati, the Rabindra-Bhavana archives still contain some of his unpublished works. Hence, if we return to the question of an ecobiography afresh, with these biographical details in mind, this comparatively new term—pertinent to the world of ecocritics—requires explanation.

Ecobiography, as a term, came into circulation due to the writings of Cecilia Konchar Farr in the 1990s, albeit in the context of the American experience. In an ecobiography, nature does not merely form the backdrop of human activities; rather, according to it, 'nature and human endeavors are less easily separated' and as 'ego and eco are inextricably intertwined… in ecobiographies nature becomes us.'[3] Rabindranath's lifelong love of nature, in the context of different places, led to a distinctive expression of the evolution of this emotion in his literary and institutional work involving Santiniketan and Sriniketan. An ecocritical reading of his career in this way literally reveals that the shaping of his life in the context of nature is inextricable from the unfolding of his creative and institutional work. In order to establish the idea of the ecobiography, Farr borrowed an important idea regarding the autobiography from Robert F. Sayre: 'The autobiographical hero is the representative of the ideas that he has lived by and seen succeed or, in some cases, fail. The autobiographer is not only a "who," he is also a "what"—what he lived for, what he believed in and worked for.'[4] Following the contours of Rabindranath's biography with the help of the ecocritical lens, we might learn about his aspirations, successes and failures in sustaining harmonious ecological relations throughout a long creative life.

Rabindranath Tagore's ecobiography aspires to present his convictions and work in the context of nature and sustainable ecological and environmental practices to a concerned global audience in the twenty-first century.

NOTES

1. The Bengali volumes are *Rabindrakabye Prani-Priti* (1991), *Madhubata Ritayate* (2005) and *Visva-Bhara Pran* (2009). The author of *Madhubata Ritayate*, Arunendu Bandyopadhyay, also wrote a monograph,

Rabindranath Tagore and Patrick Geddes: The Ecological Cultural Visionaries in 2005. Among the English essays in question are Mohit K. Ray's '*The Ramayana, Raktakarabi* and *Surfacing*: An Eco-Feminist Perspective'; Marie Josephine Aruna's "Letters' and Ecopoetics'; Amit Ray's 'Rabindranath Tagore's Vision of Ecological Harmony' and 'Tagore, Environment and Ecology: a Place-Space Dynamics'; and 'Rabindranath Tagore: An Ecocritical Reading' by Debarati Bandyopadhyay.

2. In 'Literary Studies in an Age of Environmental Crisis,' the Introduction to *The Ecocriticism Reader*, Cheryll Glotfelty wrote:

    ...as part of the definition of ecocriticism, apart from the general questions like 'How has the concept of wilderness been represented in this sonnet?' ecocriticism is engaged with issues like 'How is the environmental crisis seeping into contemporary literature and popular culture? What view of nature informs U.S. Government reports, corporate advertising, and televised nature documentaries, and to what rhetorical effect?' (xix)

    Glotfelty also wrote: '... We will see books like Aldo Leopold's *A Sand County Almanac* and Edward Abbey's *Desert Solitaire* become standard texts for courses in American literature... Ecocriticism has been predominantly a white movement' (xxv).

3. Farr, C.K. (1998). American Ecobiography. *Literature of Nature: An International Sourcebook*, 94–95.

4. Sayre, R.F. (1978). Autobiography and the Making of America. *The Iowa Review*, 150.

Introduction

Shelidah
9 August 1894

In town, human society is to the fore and looms large; it is cruelly callous to the happiness and misery of other creatures as compared with its own... When I am in close touch with Nature in the country, the Indian in me asserts itself and I cannot remain coldly indifferent to the abounding joy of life throbbing within the soft down-covered breast of a single tiny bird.

∞

Patisar
22 March 1894

How artificial is our apprehension of sin! I feel that the highest commandment is that of sympathy for all sentient beings. Love is the foundation of all religion. The other day I read in one of the English papers that 50,000 pounds of animal carcasses had been sent to some army station in Africa, but the meat being found to have gone bad on arrival, the consignment was returned and was eventually auctioned off for a few pounds at Portsmouth. What a shocking waste of life! What callousness to its true worth! How many living creatures are sacrificed only to grace the dishes at a dinner-party, a large proportion of which will leave the table untouched!

∽

Shelidah
8 May 1893

Poetry is a very old love of mine—I must have been engaged to her when I was only Rathi's age. Long ago the recesses under the old banyan tree beside our tank, the inner gardens, the unknown regions on the ground floor of the house, the whole of the outside world, the nursery rhymes and tales told by the maids, created a wonderful fairyland within me… The lover whom she favours may get his fill of bliss, but his heart's blood is wrung out under her relentless embrace… Consciously or unconsciously, I may have done many things that were untrue, but I have never uttered anything false in my poetry—that is the sanctuary where the deepest truths of my life find refuge.

—Rabindranath Tagore, *Glimpses of Bengal*[1]

Glimpses of Bengal is the translation of selected letters written by Rabindranath primarily to his niece during the late 1880s and the first few years of the 1890s from remote areas in Bengal, at a considerable distance from his family home in Calcutta. In the first excerpt, Rabindranath is a pronounced critic of the anthropocentric viewpoint. He appears to be a critic of the metropolitan culture as well, which was imperial in attitude in more than one sense. The neglect that urban people show to the well-being of living creatures other than themselves, and the repression of certain classes of human beings, should be taken into consideration in totality, in terms of these words of Rabindranath. It is also possible to imagine that Rabindranath was asserting the existence of an Indian sensibility in himself, which was not merely about his position as a colonized British subject, but about his belief that as a human being, sensitive to the Indian philosophical heritage of valuing (and not merely evaluating) all manifestations of life, he had some duties to all life forms. He also seems to suggest that this was an idea that was difficult to adhere to or remember in the modern urban environment created in India by the British masters. Within the space of a few short lines in a letter (significant in itself, because this was not fiction nor a public lecture, but an attempt to share his contemplation with a close relation, and hence, a genuine reflection of private thoughts), Rabindranath offers a critique of the role of humans in this world with respect to ecology and of the relations across species.

In the second excerpt, Rabindranath reveals a keen awareness of cruelties in his world. He highlights the irony of the situation where man has forgotten the lesson of universal love that the religion created by him espouses. The result is a powerful criticism of the modern citizens of affluent countries and imperial/military cultures from a biocentric[2] point of view.

In the third and last excerpt, Rabindranath reminisces about his childhood and comments on his life as a poet. It seems that it was his intention to establish what the nature of his relationship with poetry had been from a very early period. However, what is interesting in this description is the way he mentions the old trees and the surroundings of his ancestral house in one of the busiest sections of urban Calcutta. Just as in the earlier excerpts his sensitivity to birds and animals had been revealed, in this one, his concern for the trees and plants still surviving within a city is reflected. It could have been possible for us to dismiss his poetic sentiment as unrealistic, located close to the 'fairyland', or the land of imagination that he mentions, but for the fact that his kind of poetic sensibility required a sustained engagement with the realities of life. The deep sensibility of a poetic temperament meant that there was a constant attempt to foster kinship with all life around him. It also meant exposing himself to hurt vicariously at the sight of death, since childhood. For the literary figure that he was to become, situations that could prevent the loss of life and help an individual to feel at peace—at one with the rest of the universe—would appear to be potentially comic, while unthinking destruction would be tragic.

The lesson that Rabindranath learned about ecology came, not from the pages of dry science books, but from his own experiences and experiments in the realm of nature in the urban household of his childhood. We learn of a Calcutta in which most of the roads were unpaved and drains uncovered, and many citizens would get their drinking water from and bathe in the numerous ponds dotting the city. Rabindranath wrote[3]:

> The breast of the city of Calcutta had not been bound in stones then, it was made of dirt mostly. The sky had not turned black with the smoke from the factories. In the vacant places amidst a wilderness of edifices, there would be sun glitter on the pond water, the shadow of the fig tree would grow longer in the afternoon, the canopy of the coconut leaves would sway in the breeze.

In Calcutta, at the time, business, politics and education formed the three dominant sides of urban life as this was the capital of the British empire in India. As Rabindranath belonged to one of the most prominent families in Calcutta, his life, too, should have taken the route of education followed by a career as a landowner like his father, the sage Debendranath Tagore, or better, his illustrious grandfather, Prince Dwarkanath Tagore, who was not just a landowner, but a businessman, entrepreneur and banker acquainted with most of the royal families in Europe.

The busy hub that Calcutta was during that time in the second half of the nineteenth century seemed to have taken a backseat in Rabindranath's childhood memory though. Rather, he remembered the sudden, unexpected beauties of nature in the city. We learn significant details from the memoir of his childhood and adolescence at the Tagore family residence, titled *Chhelebela* (*My Boyhood Days*), which was written towards the end of his long life, when he looked back at the past from the vantage-point offered by old age and a rich matrix of experience[4]:

> The clock in the porch struck seven. Master Nilkamal was a stickler for punctuality, there was no chance of a moment's variation... Sitanath Datta would come, and we acquired some superficial knowledge of science... Studies of all kinds were heaped upon me, but as the burden grew greater, my mind contrived to get rid of fragments of it... I had planted a custard-apple seed in the dust which continual sweeping had collected in one corner of the verandah. All agog with excitement, I watched for the sprouting of the new leaves. As soon as Master Nilkamal had gone, I had to run and examine it, and water it. In the end my hopes went unfulfilled—the same broom that had gathered the dust together dispersed it again to the four winds.

It is possible to label Rabindranath's love for the trees and animals as romanticism. The unfulfilled childhood desire to nurture a tree can then be seen as an early manifestation of his interest in nature. It is natural for a person with a romantic temperament to love the beauty of nature for its own sake. In Rabindranath's case, the appeal of the natural surroundings outside his house, during his childhood, had a twofold significance. First, since he was not permitted to emerge from the sprawling mansion at all, there was a feeling of imprisonment; nature had remained out of his reach, adding to its charm and enigma. Second, the nature that he could not explore by himself and get acquainted with, he would try to reach through a heightening of imagination. In *Jibansmriti* (*My Reminiscences*), written when Rabindranth was about fifty years old, he recounted[5]:

> To leave the house was forbidden to us… We had to get our glimpses of nature from behind barriers. Beyond my reach stretched this limitless thing called the outside, flashes, sounds and scents of which used to come momentarily and touch me through the interstices. It seemed to want to beckon me through the shutters with a variety of gestures. But it was free and I was bound—there was no way of our meeting. So its attraction was all the stronger.

In this condition, tiny details pertaining to life in the mundane surroundings must have given him the very first lessons in ecological relations. Therefore, young Rabi recorded, on the one hand, the sight of the old tailor at one end of the veranda and the watchmen in front of the portico, and on the other, the fact that at the same spot, the horse would consume a bucketful of grain, crows would hop about pecking at the scattered chickpeas and the dog would bark at them.[6]

Human and nonhuman creatures coexisted in wholesome juxtaposition in Rabindranath's memory as an integral part of the picture of life from his childhood, even in the urban surroundings in Calcutta. Rabindranath wrote of those days when he was controlled by family servants who would imprison him within a chalk circle drawn on the floor in a room in the Jorasanko mansion. The sight, from the enclosed space, of the nature outside, would help young Rabi to relate to the world through his imagination, even though he knew he would not be permitted to reach it. The celebration of life in the activities of both human and nonhuman actors outside the boy's window had left a permanent impression of the spontaneity of ecological relations all around, in the poet's mind, for the rest of his life.

Here is another excerpt[7]:

> Just below the window of this room was a tank with a bathing ghat; on its west bank, along the garden wall, stood an immense banyan tree; and to the south was a fringe of coconut palms. Like a prisoner in a cell, I would spend the whole day peering through the closed Venetian shutters, gazing out at this scene as on a picture in a book. From early morning our neighbours would drop in one by one to take their baths. I knew the time of each one's arrival. I was familiar with the oddities of each one's toilet... [One] was in no sort of hurry at all, following a leisurely bath with a good rub-down, changing [...] then ending with a turn or two in the outer garden and the gathering of flowers, after which he would

finally saunter homewards, radiating cool comfort as he went. All this would go on till past noon. Then the bathing place would become deserted and silent. Only the ducks would remain, paddling about and diving after water snails or frantically preening their feathers, for the rest of the day... When solitude thus reigned over the water, my whole attention would focus on the shadows beneath the banyan tree. Some of its aerial roots, creeping down its trunk, had formed a dark complication of coils at its base... It was of this banyan tree that I later wrote:

Day and night you stand like an ascetic with matted hair.

Do you ever think of the boy whose fancy played with your shadows?

That majestic banyan tree is no more, alas, and neither is the tank that served as her mirror. Many of those who once bathed in it have departed too, merging with the shade of the great tree. And the boy, grown older, has put down roots far and wide and now contemplates the pattern of shadow and sunlight, sorrow and cheer, cast by the tangled skein.

The natural environment, in the vicinity of young Rabi's residence, located at the heart of Calcutta, was precious, not only as a reminder of the rural origin and tradition of the place, but also for an ecology that offered the means of sustenance and peaceful coexistence to various species of animals, birds and plants along with their human neighbours. In his record of the past, Rabindranath indicates not only a delicate consciousness of its value, but also laments that in the twentieth century, this harmony was disappearing from urban life.

The sights of treetops and the horizon combined with the call of a few birds to give him a taste of nature. With these scanty ingredients, he was eager to create a sense of being at one with nature and it is precisely this deprivation that made him most keenly aware of the real worth of all things natural. It is this childhood experience of living away from direct contact with nature that inspired Rabindranath to value every plant, animal, bird and insect, along with all the mountains, forests, rivers, seas and meadows that he had come across later in his life. In other words, so far as nature was concerned, he had learned to cherish not only the scenic beauty of it like any other person with a romantic disposition, but each and every minute aspect of life. Seeking to forge an intensely personal relation with life in all its manifestations and perpetually exploring the infinitesimal bonds that exist between the animate and inanimate aspects of the world could have formed the basis of Rabindranath's idea of life itself.

Rabindranath's first direct acquaintance with nature came when he was eleven years old. In order to escape a dengue epidemic raging in Calcutta in 1872, many members of the large family had been sent to Panihati, where they found accommodation in a house by the Ganges. The effect of this experience was to make the young boy spend hours, enraptured, by the river, imbibing, with all his senses, the world outside. It was but an obscure place in the Bengal countryside. But it offered a veritable feast of natural beauty—to him at least. This memory continued to make him marvel for many years to come, as it brought the first intimation of the realization of a deep love for nature and a natural way of life, as the foundation of his life[8]:

> This was my first outing. The bank of the Ganges welcomed me into its lap like a friend from a former birth. There [...] was a grove of guava trees; my days would pass beneath their shade, sitting on the verandah gazing at the flowing current through the gaps between the trunks. Every morning, as I awoke, I felt the day somehow coming to me like a gilt-edged letter that would impart wonderful news upon my opening the envelope... As I made fresh acquaintance with things, their dingy covering, fashioned from habit, seemed to drop away.

What is noticeable is not only his power to distil the essence of beauty from the changing aspects of the spectacle of the river at various points of time during the day even at this early age, but the ability to access, through his love of nature, the idea of a brilliant transformation of the mundane reality as if by means of defamiliarization[9].

The young boy's desire to lead his life amidst nature, away from the confines of the urban household, became the reality within a few months when his father, Maharshi Debendranath Tagore, took him first to Bolpur (Santiniketan), just after his sacred thread ceremony[10] had taken place in Jorasanko, and then to Amritsar and the western Himalayan hill station at Dalhousie to spend a few months. The sacred thread ceremony gave him a sense of the beauty of the grand sound of Sanskrit chants and, within the next few months, he was fortunate enough to learn from his father[11], the significance of the Sanskrit words in the context of nature, the Creator and the sustenance of life, especially in Dalhousie.

At this time, Rabindranath, aged eleven years and nine months, was naïve enough to believe a young relative who informed him that 'getting into a railway carriage was a terribly dangerous affair' and also that 'once aboard, a fellow had to hold on to his seat with all his might.'[12] The same Rabindranath, with the blessings of his father, became a poet and an explorer of local regions in distant countries during this journey. This tour proved to be significant for developing his power of feeling at one with all aspects of nature throughout the rest of his life. In Santiniketan, for instance, this was what he had experienced[13]:

> Though I was a mere child, my father did not place any restriction on my wanderings. In the hollows of the sandy soil the rain water had ploughed deep furrows, carving out miniature mountain ranges full of red gravel and pebbles of various shapes through

> which ran tiny streams, revealing the geography of Lilliput. From this region I would gather in the lap of my tunic many curious pieces of stone and take the collection to my father... He [...] was enthusiastic.

This atypical upbringing ensured that he would never forget to explore and appreciate the nature of any place on his own, be it famous or obscure. This had already taken him beyond the pale of the usual manifestation of romanticism. It added the dimension of a deep-rooted feeling for nature, not only in terms of those aspects visible to all others, but in terms of a finer ability not just to see and wonder, but make a place one's own in the truest sense. In Santiniketan, in the course of his explorations of the terrain, which were undertaken alone, he came across a miniature spring 'where tiny fish played and battled their way up the current' and imagined himself as the 'Livingstone of this land'; his idea that their 'water-supply' should be drawn from this spring was promptly accepted by his father and this was the crucial experience encouraging him, in future years, to make ties with nature.[14] Later, in 1901, at the age of forty, he would decide to make his father's Santiniketan Ashram, in this particular geographical area, the centre of his ecocentric educational system and existence, till his death in 1941.

Loving the natural aspects of the surroundings is, in itself, not always enough to develop a sense of one's responsibility towards either environment or ecology. It is not Rabindranath's feelings of rapture and wonder at the sight of scenic beauty that made his work—both literary and educational—worthy of this environmental-cum-literary activism. A romantic love of nature was at the root of all his work and writings. But only when it became tempered with practical considerations of the well-being of living beings breathing in a particular environment that it created texts and institutions that compel our ecocritical attention even today. If we try to follow the idea of the sanctity of life manifest in his early writings, in the order of their composition, then the preliminary form of his thought pattern regarding this becomes evident.

Rabindranath had been sent, first to Ahmedabad and then to England, when he was seventeen years old. He returned to Calcutta within sixteen months and continued to write poetry and musical drama in Bengali. His first musical play, *Valmiki-Pratibha*, staged in 1881 when he was barely twenty years old, was based on an Indian legend about the transformation of the robber-assassin Ratnakar, notorious for his bloodthirsty nature, into the poet Valmiki, who composed the great epic *Ramayana*. In Rabindranath's interpretation of the legend, Ratnakar is moved by the sudden appearance of a tiny girl in the forest. Her vulnerability inspires him to protect her from being sacrificed to Kali, the deity the robbers worshipped. Gradually, he extends this protection to the birds and animals in the forest that the other gang-members were eager to hunt and eat. When, in spite of his efforts, a bird is killed, he utters a Sanskrit couplet condemning this act and is amazed to find in himself the ability to turn emotion into poetic expression. He is then blessed by Saraswati, the goddess of erudition and artistic abilities. She appears to inform him that her visit as the little girl was necessary to awaken his humane and poetic consciousness. Subsequently, Valmiki goes on to compose the *Ramayana*. This was the transformation of Ratnakar, from a robber who left the forest awash with human and animal blood, to the poet Valmiki, with an earnest ecocentric and poetic vision that Rabindranath highlighted. This play stands as a statement of Rabindranath's own ecological consciousness too.

The next year, Rabindranath noted: 'Encouraged by the success of this new line in *Valmiki-Pratibha*, I composed another musical play of the same class. It was called *Kal Mrigaya* (*The Fateful Hunt*). The plot was based on the story in the *Ramayana* of the accidental killing of a blind hermit's only son by King Dasharatha.'[15] In this play, the young King Dasharatha had the ability to hit his target blindfolded, guided just by the slight sound a quarry might have unwittingly made. So, when he launches his arrow after hearing some sound that he believes to be made by a deer lapping up water from a river, he actually kills the young son of the blind hermit, as the boy was drawing water in an earthen vessel for his thirsty father. In the early scenes of the play, Rabindranath establishes the boy's bond with the trees and animals of the forest. Hence, the pathos of his accidental death underlines the cruelty inherent in all acts of violence.

In 1885, when he was twenty-four years old, Rabindranath wrote a story called *Rajarshi* (*The Royal Sage*) for *Balak*, a Bengali monthly for young children. In it, a king decides to stop the ancestral ritual of making blood offerings to the ruling deity of his state, when he sees a young girl trembling in fear at the prospect of such bloodshed. This is opposed by the priest, a powerful man, and the end is tragic. What is significant in the history of the composition of this novel is the revelation of the functioning of Rabindranath's sensibility during this period. He recounted that since he could not sleep during a train journey one night during this period, he thought of utilizing the time in chalking out the outline of a story for *Balak*[16]:

> In spite of my efforts a story eluded me, but sleep came to my rescue. In a dream I saw the stone steps of a temple stained with the blood of victims of sacrifice—and a little girl standing there with her father, asking him in piteous accents: 'Father, what is this, why all this blood?' and the father, inwardly moved, trying to quiet her questioning with a show of gruffness. When I awoke I felt I had got my story. Many of my stories have come to me in dreams—and other writings too. This dream episode I made part of the annals of King Gobinda Manikya of Tripura and created out of it a short serial story, *Rajarshi* (The Royal Sage) for *Balak*.

If what we learn of the inner working of the subconscious

manifesting itself in dreams is considered to be correct, then questions regarding the horror of animal sacrifice in the name of appeasing a deity—prevalent among the worshippers of Goddess Kali, a section of the Hindu society—seem to have remained submerged in Rabindranath's mind since some earlier period. The scenes depicting the young girl, Haashi (meaning 'laughter'), washing the blood off the temple steps and dying soon after in a delirious condition, are difficult to forget.

Till then, in his poetry, songs and plays, Rabindranath had not written about the hardship that human beings faced in life, in their struggle to survive in the face of a hostile nature—especially, the lower classes of people in rural society. The obvious reason for this was that till then, he had had no direct acquaintance with the hostility of nature and how human beings were affected by it. But his world was not entirely filled with natural beauty, legends and music—all of which could be appreciated only by an aristocrat spending his days in a leisurely fashion. He had witnessed lower-class life somewhat closely when he was nearly twenty-five years old: 'We were then living in a house with a garden on Lower Circular Road. Adjoining it on the south side was a large basti. I would often sit near a window and watch the goings-on in this populous settlement. I loved to see the inhabitants work, play and rest, and come and go multifariously. To me it was like a story come alive.'[17] Rabindranath's description reveals that at this stage, he had not understood the pathos of the slum-dwellers' life. He viewed them quite simply as human beings, and not compulsorily as unfortunate or suffering human beings. Therefore, he could still continue to write about and have nightmares of the bloodshed of animals. Awakening to the reality of the rural population's struggle for survival became necessary before Rabindranath could think and write with maturity, about the exigencies of human life, economy and also nature.

NOTES

1. Tagore, R. *Glimpses of Bengal. Fullbooks.*
2. According to the Oxford Dictionary, biocentricism is 'The view or belief that the rights and needs of humans are not more important than those of other living things.' Both biocentricism and ecocentricism oppose human-oriented approaches. Whereas the former takes into consideration individual organisms, the latter takes the entire ecosystem into account.
3. Pal, P. K. (1982). *Rabijibani* [Biography of Rabindranath Tagore]. Vol. 1, 31. (The translation provided here is by Debarati Bandyopadhyay).
4. Tagore, R. 'My Boyhood Days' *Rabindranath Tagore Omnibus 1*. 816–17
5. Tagore, R. *My Reminiscences*. 13
6. Tagore, R. *Boyhood Days* 45.
7. Tagore, R. 'From *My Reminiscences*' *Rabindranath Tagore: An Anthology*, 58–59.
8. *My Reminiscences*, 42–43.
9. According to David Lodge's *The Art of Fiction*: 'Defamiliarization is the usual English translation of ostranenie (literally, 'making strange')… In

a famous essay first published in 1917, Victor Shklovsky argued that the essential purpose of art is to overcome the deadening effects of habit by representing familiar things in unfamiliar ways. Habitualization devours works, clothes, furniture, one's wife, and the fear of war… And art exists that one may recover the sensation of life; it exists to make one feel things, to make the stone *stony*.' (53)

10. Sacred thread ceremony is a ritual that preadolescent Brahmin boys undergo, which indicates their second birth.
11. Maharshi Debendranath was the leader of the Brahmo Samaj, which was based on the teachings of the Upanishads. Rabindranath had the best possible teacher in his father, who would wake him up before sunrise to teach him and help him feel at one with the universe.
12. Tagore, R. *My Reminiscences*. 76
13. Ibid., 78.
14. Ibid., 79–80.
15. Ibid., 185.
16. Ibid., 232–33.
17. Ibid., 229.

Chapter 1

The Storm:
Glimpses of Bengal and *Gora*

Rabindranath experienced nature as the source of beauty and spiritual solace in the early part of his life. A heightened aesthetic perception appears to have combined with the teachings of his father, Maharshi Debendranath Tagore, to give him this sense of the world and the beauty underlying it. The fact that nature could also be the cause of untold hardship in the human world, as a great many people continued to depend on it for bare survival, does not seem to have found much reflection in his writings earlier. However, his romantic nature received a jolt in mid-1885 when due to a drought for two consecutive years, there was a dreadful famine in the districts of Bankura, Birbhum and parts of Burdwan, in Bengal. The British government did not provide adequate assistance. The poor people in these areas continued to suffer. Rabindranath led an effort to collect donations for the area on 12 April 1885, during a special meeting of the Adi Brahma Samaj, on the eve of the auspicious occasion of the Bengali New Year. The poet made an impassioned appeal to his Bengali brethren[1]:

> Not too far—it is close to your doors that the hungry people stand. They look with such craving at the leftovers that you throw to the cats and dogs every day! You rejoice in the birth of a son; their starving infant does not even have the strength to cry. You celebrate a wedding at home; and lack of just a handful of rice results in the permanent disbanding of their marriage-bond—providing his wife with food is the ultimate duty that the husband fails to perform. You sit serene at home, talk matters over, feel amused, concentrate on family affairs; they have no other topic, thought or work—in their life, all thoughts, all the desires of their heart and all their hopes, day and night, remain bound to a handful of rice…
>
> Hunger is such a terrible hazard, yet a lot of us fail to picture it. Various other kinds of danger awaken humanity in human beings—but hunger makes them inhuman…
>
> … Indeed, don't you have anything? Are you more destitute than the one who has only had boiled tamarind seeds as grain during the last few days? For the last three days, one has been chewing on the dry roots of the sugarcane, barely moistening it; can't you

help even him? Possibly this is what is going on in your mind—'If the scores of affluent people do not help the poor victims, what can be there for us to do!' Don't say such things. Cruelty means withdrawal into the self. The stone that does not feel any pain might continue to thrive in a state of apathy, yet you should not imitate this and be like it…

Rabindranath donated ₹500 first and then asked others for their contribution to the relief work. He proposed to rehabilitate these farmers and their families to the Tagore family estate in the Sunderbans, but none showed any interest.[2]

Rabindranath was the progeny of a family of landowners who had prospered consistently. The only exception had been a financial setback after the sudden demise of Prince Dwarkanath Tagore, abroad. But Maharshi Debendranath, his sage-like eldest son, had worked long and hard to repay all the debts, and the family had prospered again. Like the other children in the family, Rabindranath had led a very simple life in his childhood. But this was by no means due to poverty. While the wealthy section of citizens in India could afford to help the poor and needy, perhaps not many could feel their sorrow keenly. There does not seem to have been much of a chance in the early part of his life for Rabindranath to learn about the hardships of the rural population. But he reveals an immediate intuitive understanding of their socio-economic condition by the mid-1880s. There is also the case of the excellent forethought that prompted him to offer the drought-stricken farmers land for cultivation and houses for their families in the Sunderbans. And this is, by no means, a singular instance of his concern for the rural poor, largely neglected by the urban elite in British India. Rather, in *Glimpses of Bengal*, we learn about the foundation of his endeavour to work towards the improvement of those circumstances that affected the rural people who depended on nature for their livelihood, and whose voices were not generally heard or represented in polite circles. The only notable exceptions were the sporadic newspaper reports about the oppressed farmers at indigo plantations in India, including vast parts of Bengal; and the publication of Dinabandhu Mitra's play *Nil Darpan* on the same subject, which faced retaliation by the British after its translation into English.

During the late 1880s and till the mid-1890s, the period during which Rabindranath had written *Glimpses of Bengal*, he had been entrusted with the task of supervising the family estate (some of these places are now part of Bangladesh). He resided, for the most part, in Shilaidaha (variously spelt; for instance, in *Glimpses of Bengal*, we find 'Shelidah'), Shajadpur, Patisar and Kaligram.

Rabindranath wrote a series of letters in Bengali to a sophisticated and highly accomplished young lady, Indira Devi, the daughter of his second eldest brother,

Satyendranath Tagore, who was the first Indian to enter the Indian Civil Service (ICS) through the competitive exams in London. She copied these letters in her exercise books and resubmitted the whole to the writer himself; Rabindranath selected 145 letters, and edited and published these as *Chhinnapatra* in 1912. One hundred and seven more letters, as well as sections of letters left out from *Chhinnapatra*, were published in the bigger compilation, *Chhinnapatravali*, much later in 1960, by Visva-Bharati. In Sanskrit and Bengali, 'chhinna' suggests torn and 'patra' suggests both leaves and letters. Rabindranath decided to get selected letters from *Chhinnapatra* translated into English as *Glimpses of Bengal: Selected from the Letters of Sir Rabindranath Tagore 1885 to 1895*, and this was published in 1921. In the introduction to *Glimpses of Bengal*, Rabindranath wrote:

> Since these letters synchronize with a considerable part of my published writings, I thought their parallel course would broaden my readers' understanding of my poems as a track is widened by retreading the same ground... Hoping that the descriptions of village scenes in Bengal contained in these letters would also be of interest to English readers, the translation of a selection has been entrusted to one who, among all those whom I know, was best fitted to carry it out.

This bears the date 20 June 1920, which suggests that Rabindranath, in hindsight, possibly felt it necessary to share some of the personal letters written in the nineteenth century with his readers in the twentieth century. Incidentally, he entrusted the translation of *Chhinnapatra* to his nephew Surendranath Tagore, the elder brother of the original addressee of these letters, Indira Devi. In these letters, initially there is a sentimental depiction of the beauty of the land and water, and the people living close to nature, in the countryside. This has been conveyed in a tone that transports the reader far away from the furious pace of activities in cities and towns to what seems like a rather indolent world. Yet, reading Rabindranath's letters to his niece chronologically, we come across evidence of his gradual and complete realization of the suffering of the rural people who were thoroughly dependent upon the bounties of nature for their survival and sustenance.

In the remote areas in Bengal, Rabindranath was compelled to understand the anxiety of the peasants who sought the kindness of the same natural elements he used to romanticize earlier. In *Glimpses of Bengal*, in a letter written on 10 May 1893 from Shelidah, to his niece, who was living in the fashionable British hill town of Shimla at the time, Rabindranath says: 'Here come black, swollen masses of cloud… Over there, on the sky-piercing peaks of Simla, you will find it hard to realize exactly what an important event the coming of clouds is here, or how many are anxiously looking up to the sky, hailing their advent.'

Rabindranath also gradually became aware of some of the central paradoxes governing the lives of the poor people relying on nature. These farmers would pray to nature to be merciful and generous. This community depended on the fertile land of the lower Gangetic delta that produced paddy in large quantities. Rice was their staple food and means of survival. On the one hand, little or no rain caused drought, and on the other, too much rain led to flooding—both resulting in famine and starvation. At this stage, Rabindranath seemed to have recognized the extent of their poverty and the reasons behind this situation. In the letter dated 10 May 1893, he also wrote: 'I feel a great tenderness for these peasant folk—our ryots[3]—big, helpless, infantile children of providence, who must have food brought to their very lips, or they are undone. When the breasts of Mother Earth dry up, they are at a loss what to do, and can only cry.' It was his sympathy that prompted Rabindranath to view the villagers as helpless in any situation involving a problem in the natural environment. Rabindranath was well aware that the villagers did not live in a prelapsarian world. There were social rifts and quarrels and we find a reflection of some of these situations in his fictional works, such as *Gora, Home and the World* and a number of short stories that are set in rural Bengal. Yet, in these, and in the letters of *Chhinnapatra*, we find a sincere concern for the illiterate peasants' dependence on nature and their vulnerability in this matter.

Rabindranath's thoughtfulness for the villagers is not a mere mark of a rich landowner's benevolence. Zamindars (landowners) were generally indifferent to the troubles of the tenants or peasants. Often, these zamindars would live off the produce of the land and lead a life of luxury in Calcutta. In contrast, Rabindranath supervised his father's estate with real anxiety at the sight of the villagers' suffering. His concern does not appear to be born of merely a predilection for romanticism. The rest of the letter (10 May 1893) in *Glimpses of Bengal* indicates that his concern for the rural population was due to a sound understanding of economics, public policy and ecological relations:

> They say a terribly hard thing, who assert that the division of the world's production to afford each one a mouthful of food, a bit of clothing, is only an Utopian dream. All these social problems are hard indeed! Fate has allowed humanity such a pitifully meagre coverlet, that in pulling it over one part of the world, another has to be left bare.

This letter no longer indicates the sentimental side of Rabindranath. Rather, he clearly critiques the economic basis of the relationship between nature and human beings. Nature can be viewed as the Earth-Mother who nourishes us, as in any traditional worldview. It is also interpreted in the modern world as the ultimate repository of resources and this viewpoint suggests a competition for its quick and efficient exploitation. A very basic idea related to economics is that natural resources are limited but human desire and greed are not. Those who grab these resources early and use them efficiently for a long time, continue to rule. Naturally, they also try to leave the rest of the people in a position where they cannot even compete for the same riches. In contrast, in terms of Deep Ecology in our times, looking at nature with an intention to make use of it is absolutely wrong, as nature is not just a vast repository of resources; rather, each and every little stream, hill, clod and even an apparently insignificant insect has the full right to exist freely, without any obligation to serve human interests. Rabindranath, a hundred years ago, appears to have understood that land and water resources were being sought desperately by an extremely poor section of the human population. However, there are others who continue to utilize natural resources ravenously and indiscriminately to maximize profit, causing a crisis even in remote rural areas, for instance, Bengal. He commiserates with the rural poor, and criticizes the rich exploiters of nature, unequivocally. A few years from the writing of this letter, we find a reflection of his estimate of the rapacious nature of the rich and the abuse of this land by the powerful, or, in other words, the nexus of economy and politics ruining natural and human existence, in *Gora*. Though *Gora* was published in 1910, it is set in the last decades of the nineteenth century, or the period when, roughly speaking, Rabindranath was beginning to learn about the land and the people.

In the letters written to his niece Indira, Rabindranath related his reading of the deplorable condition of the farmers quite consistently and emphasized the nature of their vulnerability[4]:

The river has entered our char-land. The farmers are heaping their boats with green paddy. I continue to hear their anguished cries as their boats pass by mine. You will understand that it is heart-rending for them to reap the crop at a time when it would have ripened properly if only it could stand for a few more days. Their utmost hope is to find a few ripened ears of grain in that lot… The supplication of hundreds of thousands of wretched, inoffensive creatures does not seem to get anywhere—it continues to pour, the river continues to rise, and no relief seems to be forthcoming from any quarter.

During a period when the greater part of the cultured Bengalees as well as the learned, sophisticated urban Indians were largely oblivious to the suffering of human beings who had to surrender completely to nature, Rabindranath's expression of empathy for them remained an exception. From a romantic poet worshipping the beauty of nature, he appeared to be well set to transform himself into a socially aware human being who really felt the sorrow of the people on the margins. If we remember the history of the majority of zamindars exploiting the peasants for the sake of earning higher revenues, Rabindranath's views regarding the same section of people in the society, and his grasp of the pathos and paradox of the situation prove to be remarkable. He wrote in a letter: 'I was struck with shame that I was a zamindar, impelled by the money motive, absorbed in revenue returns.'[5] However, his letters and short stories make it clear that he was never a mere 'zamindar' who was interested in making money. Rather, it is this money-making motive that is critiqued in his literary work. His son Rathindranath's memoir, *On the Edges of Time* (1958), provides proof that Rabindranath was neither a coercive landowner, nor merely a literary figure who would live in seclusion and spin webs of fiction, drama and poetry. Rathindranath highlighted the dual aspect of his father's life as a prolific literary artist and efficient manager during this period and, in the process, revealed[6]:

> In spite of his heavy literary work, Father did not neglect his managerial duties. Every morning he would go through the accounts, hear reports from the staff, and dispose of important correspondence. But the most interesting function for him was to meet the tenants, hear their complaints and settle disputes. He did not treat them in the traditional manner. He talked with them freely and they too felt so much at ease with him that they would tell him about their land, their families, and their personal affairs. Father had made known that any tenant who wanted to see him could go straight to him: no officer was to interfere with this inherent right of the tenant.

The contrast between Rabindranath's privileged social position and his spontaneous sympathy with the people living on the margins, make the letters and stories critically and historically interesting, as documentation of a rare capacity to feel and act as a conscientious individual towards both human and natural existence[7]:

> Throughout his life, Tagore communicated with family, friends, public figures and professional associates through letters that constitute a veritable treasure trove of social commentary, self-revelation, philosophical meditation, and literary creativity. Unlike other literary genres, letters occupy the borderline between public and private worlds. Tagore's letters reveal facets of his personality that do not emerge from his formal writings and speeches.

It is this idea of letters occupying the borderline between one's public statements and a personal utterance that is important, especially while reading *Chhinnapatra*. We learn about Rabindranath, the shy man discharging his duties amongst ignorant villagers far away from the elite society of Calcutta and, in the process, educating himself by 'reading' this land and its people with utmost care.

At this juncture, Rabindranath seems to abhor the idea that those with power—physical, financial or political—would appropriate natural resources and products quickly and those lacking it would continue to live in a dehumanized condition, and starve and perish in floods and droughts silently. The romantic poet could have chosen to make an escape from the world of their palpable sorrow into the beauty of nature, and he craved for this solace during the period. In a letter to Pramatha Chaudhuri (brother of his friend Asutosh; Pramatha would marry his niece, Indira, who regularly received the *Chhinnapatra* letters from him during the same period), Rabindranath, in 1891, wrote from Sajadpur: 'At present, there are times when I feel a conflict of two opposite forces within myself... Poetry on one side and philosophy on another... Attachment for work on one hand and the attraction of thought on the other... I wish to view myself objectively through you all.[8]

The next year too, Rabindranath wrote to Pramatha on 19 December 1892, from Shilaidaha, about the same conflict[9]:

> Writing poetry has perforce been my lifelong intoxication... I think of completing as many tasks as possible at one go so as to concentrate on my poem at ease, in peace and seclusion—but each and every day and month arrives with its new tasks—there is none to extend help, taking pity on me... But the ideal of my life is not to ignore but to shoulder patiently any burden that comes my way... Hence every month, with a bowed head, I continue to write for Bharati and every day, work with utmost concentration on the petty details of the zamindari. Do you think that this gives me any pleasure?... Riding on the pegasus called imagination is not a good exercise for my mind.

Presumably, the gravity of reality pulled him back from the realms of imagination. He paid homage to Mother Nature but also felt constrained to accuse her as the origin of disasters in the lives of poor villagers who depended on her completely for subsistence. He was also showing his growing awareness of issues related to inequity in the economy and social relations during the same period, in the short stories and the *Chhinnapatravali* letters. Krishna Kripalani, as Rabindranath's biographer, has viewed this phase of his life as extremely significant[10]:

> ... [H]e had to [...] look after the interests of the family estates and adjust them, as best as he could, to the welfare of the tenants... He not only needed this discipline to make a man of him, but the years he thus spent in the heart of rural Bengal widened and strengthened his intimacy with nature which he loved and provided glimpses into the varied landscape of his country which he might not otherwise have known. This was rich food for his poetry.
>
> But even richer were the insights he gained into the life of the common people, their daily drudgery and constant struggle against the freaks of nature, the callous indifference of landlords, the no less callous indifference of a rigid social orthodoxy and of an alien political rule... the social and economic conditions which had crippled the scope of these lives. This [...] provided the backbone to his success as a short-story writer and to his understanding of his country's social and economic ills. The letters he wrote during this period [...] are a testament to his widening sympathies

as a man… As they were not intended for publication, he wrote freely and without any self-consciousness. They provide not only glimpses of Bengal but also glimpses of the author's own development.

Chronologically speaking, the years during which Rabindranath was writing the letters of *Chhinnapatravali* were also the period of the composition of many of his famous short stories that depict the abysmal suffering of the rural population at the time of droughts or floods. The muddy, waterlogged and unhealthy environment of the villages, which became the breeding ground of malaria and enteric diseases, causing death across generations, have been mentioned consistently in these stories. The result of making new acquaintances in the rural society during this period was that Rabindranath could write a story like 'The Postmaster', through which we are transported to the village of Ulapur where a young man from Calcutta, who arrives as the Postmaster, 'felt like a fish out of water in this remote village.'[11] He does not like the company of the villagers and the workers in the factory adjacent to the village. However, his immediate response of seeking an escape from the physical conditions of Ulapur serves as an index to the average townsman's shock at encountering an obscure part of one's own country. Rabindranath, in 'The Postmaster,' described this early view of Ulapur as: 'His office and living-room were in a dark thatched shed, not far from a slimy pond, surrounded on all sides by a dense growth'[12]. Soon, a fever prompts him to request a transfer 'on the ground of the unhealthiness of the place.'[13] It is rejected. He, thus, resigns and leaves.

Rabindranath, though living in the family mansion or the big boat on the river during his stewardship of the family estate, appears to have noted the trials and tribulations that the average urban man would undergo in any village. He arouses sympathy for the Postmaster. And yet, we are left with the impression that the villagers, like the young maidservant Ratan, whom the Postmaster leaves behind, continue to suffer in the same unhygienic conditions. The urban man makes his escape, but the rural woman cannot.

On 30 November 1891, the inaugural issue of *Sadhana*, the magazine published by the Tagore family, carried Rabindranath's short story 'Khokabaur Pratyabartan,' translated as 'The Child's Return'. In this story, Anukul 'was transferred to a district on the banks of the Padma.'[14] He was there on judiciary service, accompanied by his wife, son and Raicharan, the loyal servant. Following is an excerpt[15]:

> Then came the rainy season, and day after day, the rain poured down. The hungry river, like an enormous serpent, swallowed terraces, villages, and corn-fields, covering with its flood the tall grasses and wild casuarinas on the sandbanks. From time to time there was a deep thud as the river-banks crumbled.

The overflowing river was a potent agent of destruction of lives and livelihoods in remote parts of Bengal but in the story, this dangerous situation is acknowledged by the educated citizens only when Anukul's tiny son is swallowed by the river.

Within three years of the composition of these two stories, during the period of the writing of the *Chhinnapatravali* letters, in 'Megh o Roudra' (Cloud and Sun), Rabindranath highlighted the rural folk's affinity with the river and their exploitation by the British, through the experiences of the young lawyer Sashibhushan, who lived in a village and sympathized with the villagers[16]:

> A new steamer line had recently been opened from the station landing-place to the district-town… The young Manager Sahib of the new line and a few passengers were on board, among whom were some inhabitants of Sashibhushan's village.
>
> A [...] country-boat was trying to race the steamer from a little way off; at times it seemed about to catch up with her… The boatman's spirit of rivalry was awakened… The boat plunged forward like a horse with its reins snapped. At a certain point the path of the steamer took a slight bend, and here the boat outstripped it by taking a shorter cut… [J]ust then the Sahib raised his revolver and fired a shot at the swollen sail. In a moment the sail burst, the boat sank… the man who was grinding spices for cooking [...] could not be traced. The rain-swollen river flowed on swiftly.

Sashibhushan rescued the rest of the boatmen because his boat was the nearest. However, he also turned out to be the only eyewitness, who wanted to take the necessary legal step to bring justice to the victims. The narrator comments on the nature of this act of unpremeditated cruelty[17]:

> Why the Manager acted thus, it is difficult to say... Perhaps he felt the rivalry of an Indian sail to be intolerable... But this I know for certain that the Englishman believed he would not be liable to be punished for this little joke, and he had an idea that the people whose boat was lost and who were in danger of losing their lives also could not be counted as human beings.

Rabindranath's tone conveys the indifference of the British officials towards the survival and welfare of the common citizens, especially the illiterate villagers. Ironically, when Sashibhushan urges the boatman to file a police case against the Manager for the loss of a life and a boat laden with jute, the simple man proves to be mortally afraid of the law, the court and the police. He expresses a terror of the hassles and the coercive treatment that would prove doubly harmful, in case he decides to seek justice. Equally ironical is the refusal of the people of Sashibhushan's village to bear witness. They proclaim to have been at the back of the steamer and hence unable to see or hear anything as momentous as a gunshot. The climax is reached when Sashibhushan persuades the boatman to bring the matter before the magistrate, promising to shoulder every burden, financial or otherwise, for the sake of justice, though the Manager simply negates his efforts[18]:

> No witnesses were required. The Manager admitted he had fired a shot. He said it was aimed at a flock of cranes flying in the sky. The steamer was then going at full speed and had just turned round the bend. So he could not possibly know whether a crow died or a crane died or the boat sank. Earth and sky contained so many things to aim at that no man in his senses would knowingly waste a pice-worth of shot on a dirty rag.

This last part proves to be the masterstroke. It convinces the Magistrate effectively that the Manager could never have intended to harm the poor boatmen, and that the entire thing was just an accident. Rabindranath had the nerve to publish stories criticizing the travesty of justice and fair play for the vulnerable sections of Indians, living on the margins of the British empire. He was, by birth, far superior, even to prosperous and educated villagers like Sashibhushan in the story. Yet, the indignation becomes palpable even in translation. His narrative tone in 'Cloud and Sun' echoes Sashibhushan's disappointment[19]:

> Acquitted on all charges, the Manager Sahib, puffing at a cigar, went to play whist at his club. The dead body of the man who was grinding spices in the boat was washed up on land nine miles farther off, and

Sashibhushan returned to his village with frustration raging in his breast.

In 'Cloud and Sun', Sashibhushan, without thinking of his own safety and career at all, later protests yet again when he sees acts of exploitation and injustice. He should have understood that the villagers, both known and unknown to him, would not dare to raise their voice to protest against the British people's acts of coercion and injustice even when it meant the destruction of their lives and livelihoods. Educated citizens too, are shown as loyal to the British Empire, who would, for the most part, instinctively prefer to avoid trouble even if their hapless compatriots required urgent help. It is also quite possible that these educated Indians living in towns and cities like Calcutta would not learn anything about the rural incidents, till any of these found a reference in some newspaper report. It is ironical that in the story, each villager appears to ignore the possibility that the same fate might await him too. Rabindranath deliberately highlights the imaginary Sashibhushan's near suicidal attempts at helping the marginalized people. The next attempt of Sashibhushan came equally spontaneously. He protests against the District Superintendent of Police who destroyed the large fishing net of a group of fishermen. The victims were mortally afraid of police retaliation and preferred to remain silent. Sashibhushan's intervention earns him five years' imprisonment. But what did he do to merit such a punishment? Why did he have to intervene at all?

The fishermen had fixed bamboo-poles on either side of the confluence of two rivers and spread a huge net over them, keeping only room on one side for boats to pass. They had been doing this since a long time, and also paying rent for it. As ill luck would have it, this year the august District Superintendent of Police had suddenly deigned to come this way. Seeing his boat draw near, the fishermen warned his boatman beforehand in a loud voice and pointed out the passage at the side. But the Sahib's boatman was not in the habit of showing deference to any man-made barrier by taking a roundabout route, so he steered the boat clean through the net. The net stooped and made way for the boat, but its rudder became enmeshed and it took some time and trouble to disentangle it.

The Police Sahib got extremely red and angry, and had the boat moored. The four fishermen, seeing his threatening attitude, promptly decamped. The Sahib ordered his oarsmen to cut up the net, and the huge net, made at a cost of seven or eight hundred rupees, was cut to pieces.[20]

Sashibhushan hurries to the Sahib from his boat anchored nearby, to point out the injustice of this act, and the Sahib insults him by using a dirty expletive that makes him strike the man. It is as a result of this crime that he finds himself thoroughly beaten up and imprisoned. However, this story of Sashibhushan's repeated protest against others' misdeeds remains highly significant from the perspective of both postcolonialism and ecocriticism. As a citizen of India—which was a British colony at the time of the composition of this story—Rabindranath clearly had two choices. The scion of the Tagore family could easily live in Calcutta, or he could stay in England and have a very nice relationship with the British officials. The alternative was to keep his eyes open and think of the country not as an agglomeration of mountains, rivers, fields and trees that inspired poetic compositions, but in terms of the soil, the water and the people, for whom a humane concern would gradually become a very important focal point in his life. Ecocritics in general, and postcolonial ecocritics and ecofeminists in particular, concentrate on the intersection of the exploitation of nature and the marginalized sections of the population usually living closest to it. The Sahib's proclamation that he aims to kill a bird in the 'Cloud and Sun' appears to be unassailable. The fact that human beings hunt animals and birds appears to be quite natural. Similarly, the white master's power over both nature and the natives in India appears to be a matter of right. This is the attitude that current postcolonial and ecocritical readings of the situation would criticize; Rabindranath had written the story more than a hundred years ago!

In the process of protesting, Sashibhushan incurs the wrath of the British officials and his own countrymen shun him too, not wanting to get involved in any kind of trouble. We can understand their motives. But Rabindranath refuses to give Sashibhushan any personal reason or selfish motive for his attempts to bring justice to the victims. He is not involved in politics. He is not an urban man visiting the villages. He is not a member of the Congress, though this is the label that is easily appended to him the moment he is identified as a troublemaker, in front of the British Magistrate. Rabindranath portrays Sashibhushan as a village youth with a degree in law. He is somewhat shortsighted and, therefore, frowns to see and read correctly. In other words, it is possible that Rabindranath wanted to show that Sashibhushan's acts of spontaneous protest and sacrifice of time, energy, money and social position for others are not tainted by any economic or financial motive. Why, then, did Rabindranath depict the misadventures of this nondescript person with such sympathetic care? And why did Indira, the recipient of the letters in *Chhinnapatra*, choose to translate this story from Bengali to English? Much later, in a lecture delivered in China in 1924 and published as 'Civilization and Progress,' he commented[21]:

> I have read somewhere an observation of Plato in which he says: 'An intelligent and socialized community will continue to grow only as long as it can remain a unit; beyond that point growth must cease, or the community will disintegrate and cease to be an organic being.' That spirit of the unit is only maintained when its nucleus is some living sentiment of dharma, leading to cooperation and to a common sharing of life's gifts.

Is it not possible, then, to view Rabindranath's idea of the organic nature of the community and the 'living sentiment' as basic to the idea of a sustainable ecological relationship, the inspiration behind ecocritical work today, considering the fact that the words ecology, economy and ecocriticism are derived from 'oikos' in Greek, which means 'household' or—perhaps, even better— 'home'? Is it possible that the author considered reiterating, in fiction, the contrast between the fragmented, self-divided condition of the village society and the solitary man's selfless vigil, necessary to awaken the conscience of the Indians reading the story? In this sense it could be related to Gora from his famous novel of the same name, Nikhil from *The Home and the World*, and in fact, Rabindranath himself, who was, all along, painstakingly attempting to get to know about the villagers and traversing a lonely path to seek justice and subsistence for them. It was, perhaps, the only humane and decent course of action that he could imagine during this period.

In *Gora*, Rabindranath took great care to show the transformation of an urban man who did not know about the pathetic condition of the land and the people into a dedicated soul tirelessly working for both. This forms the crux of the quest for meaning, in individual, national and earthly existence. The way to the heart of Gora's being—his idea of 'Bharatbarsha' or the true India; the object of his quest—could only pass through the villages where rural people had lost not only their land or a harvest of paddy, but also the fertility of the soil, and where almost all the adult men were imprisoned and the women abused, for the sake of the cash crop, indigo. The bright colour of the dye kept hidden the real history of the robbery of the soil and the lives of the people in India.

Historically speaking, indigo plantations in Bengal and parts of eastern India in the nineteenth century became a site of contention between the (mostly) white planters and the ryots who had been living and working in the villages for generations. The planters, intending to maximize their profit, compelled the men to work only on indigo. The victims were not only beaten and imprisoned, and the women in their families ravished, but the tracts of land on which they had earlier produced paddy, would now be used only for indigo, resulting in a supposed scarcity of food and further suffering in the hands of the masters. Dinabandhu Mitra's *Nil Darpan* was a significant play in Bengali that protested against the atrocities of the indigo planters. The British indigo planters put a ban on the performance of the play, which had been happening for decades. They even put the publisher of the English translation of *Nil Darpan* on trial. These incidents revealed the reactionary nature of the British and failure of the Indians at building up some resistance to the indigo planters. Even in *Gora*, set in the nineteenth century, there is an episode in which the protagonist encounters British oppression due to his protest against indigo cultivation in an obscure part of Bengal called Char Ghoshpur. Both *Nil Darpan* and the Char Ghoshpur episode in *Gora* are of momentous importance not only for the socio-economic history of Bengal and India, but also their cultural history. Rabindranath himself was born one year after the publication of *Nil Darpan*.

While Rabindranath was writing about indigo, the planters and the Indian peasants from an oppressed Indian's perspective, the British man's view too would be necessary to establish the historical context of nineteenth-century Bengal. In an article, 'Indigo Planting in India', published in the *Pearson's Magazine* in 1900, one M.N. MacDonald has eloquently praised the beauty and efficacy of indigo prepared in India[22]:

> Indigo, the most beautiful and expensive of all dyes in common use, has ever been closely related to India, as its name implies.
>
> From India the ancient Greeks and Romans drew supplies of the blue dye, and although it was lost to Europe during the greater part of the Middle Ages, enormous quantities have been imported for commercial purposes during the last hundred years. Today, nearly all blue uniforms of our Navy and Army, and policemen and postmen, are dyed with the purest natural indigo, which resist bad weather and sea-water better than any other dye. For similar purposes, the United States demand as large a quantity as we do, while France, Germany, Italy, and Russia are also extensive buyers of the Indian blue.

In view of the extensive demand of Indian indigo in the international arena, it was clearly for the benefit of the owners of indigo plantations and factories that the British Government too, took considerable interest in the whole business. MacDonald noted[23]:

> Indigo is cultivated all over India, giving employment to millions of natives and thousands of Englishmen. In three districts alone, in Behar, where some of the finest indigo is grown, European capital is invested to the extent of no less than £5,000,000. Some 370,000 acres are under cultivation. There are seven hundred English gentlemen managing and working on the 'concerns'—as the factories and plantation are always called—and 1,500,000 natives. As a rule, the concerns are under English management.

MacDonald complained that the natives always tried to cheat in the cultivation of indigo. A few British masters subduing and controlling a large number of native workers was natural, according to MacDonald, considering the substantial British gains from the business: 'The manufacturer, having made indigo, sends samples to the brokers at Calcutta [...] the central market for all India, and sales are held here from December to February, agents coming to buy from New York, London, and the European capitals... In 1877, 61,000 cwt. were sent to the United States.'[24] MacDonald did not mention the coercive measures adopted to make native peasants cultivate indigo under duress for months and the way they were whipped and starved to ensure compliance. Rather, he wrote: 'In May and June, when all the country is parched and scorched, the indigo fields are a mass of waving green, very pleasant and restful to the eye. Towards the end of June [...] the crop is cut [...] in September a second crop is taken...sometimes three crops are taken in one season.'[25]

The congratulatory and complacent words do not even once mention that the intensive use of land for indigo cultivation meant that the Indian peasants would not have much opportunity to grow food crops necessary for their subsistence. We also learn that planting indigo would eventually destroy the fertility of the soil. In a direct contrast to MacDonald's praise of indigo, in 1989, we learnt from the noted ecofeminist Vandana Shiva, how planting of eucalyptus today can be compared with the harmful effects of indigo plantation in the nineteenth century[26]:

> Most environment movements in India are responses of the people to exploitation of common resources for the privileges of a few... In Karnataka recently, a major movement has emerged called the 'Mannu Rakshana Koota' or save the soil campaign, which is a popular reaction against government policy to put eucalyptus on farmlands and pastures. Eucalyptus depletes soil fertility and destroys water resources. The people's hunger for food and thirst for water is being sacrificed in government development planning to satisfy the raw material hunger of the pulp industry...
>
> The movement against eucalyptus has a number of

parallels with the first Gandhian struggle against indigo plantation which became famous as the Champaran Satyagraha. Indigo was an important dye for the British textile industry just as the eucalyptus is an important raw material for the pulp industry.

To ecocritics, then, the environmental history of India has had catastrophic moments, and the plantation of indigo formed a defining moment in this chronicle.

Returning to 1900, we find that MacDonald's presentation of the indigo plantations and factories was uncritically enthusiastic. Reading his account renders it impossible for the readers to understand the Indian farmers' and workers' extreme suffering in the hands of the British indigo planters, which ultimately caused the indigo revolt[27]:

…indigo gradually became significant for Englishmen in India as a chief means of remittance whereby profits could be translated into British currency. This encouraged extravagant speculation in indigo, especially by the Union Bank of Calcutta during the period 1829 to 1847. In the later year the bank collapsed, leading to the bankruptcy of many planters. They tried to resuscitate their business [...] by extraordinary exploitation of the peasantry... The evangelical and liberal Governor-General, William Bentinck, for example, viewed British planters as civilizing agents who should be given legal protection and encouragement. This attitude fostered the subtle spread of planter oppression... In actuality, almost all these officials bent over backward to use recent emergency legislation in favour of planters. This legislation—Act XI of 1860 [...] reinforced the ability of planters to demand fulfilment of indigo contracts during the current season... Of all the magistrates in Lower Bengal, only one 'measured up to the high standards usually associated with the Indian Civil Service'.

Chronologically speaking, Dinabandhu Mitra (1829–74) was Rabindranath's senior by decades and a representative of an earlier batch of enlightened Bengali gentlemen. He is historically evaluated as one who was able to draw the attention of city dwellers to rural suffering[28]:

> Dinabandhu Mitra's native place Jessore was one of the worst affected regions, and he had good information as well as his own experience. He wrote his first play *Nil-darpan* (*An Indigo Mirror*, Dacca, 1860) giving a grim picture of inhuman villainy and torture... as a gripping stage play it was effective, and it went a long way towards the suppression of the evil... For its propaganda value *Nil-darpan* belongs to the same class of effective books as *Uncle Tom's Cabin*, *Nicholas Nickleby* and *Oliver Twist*.

Nil Darpan was translated into English by Michael Madhusudan Dutt (1824–73) in 1869 as *Nil Durpan or The Indigo Planting Mirror*. Reverend James Long, the publisher, was tried and punished by the British Government.

Rabindranath's novel, *Gora*, was published in Bengali in 1910, the period when the ban on performances of Mitra's play had barely been lifted. However, both Rabindranath and Gora remained immersed in contemporary sociocultural problems. It is a part of Bengal that the author and the character visit in the latter part of the nineteenth century and evaluate personally[29]:

> Gora [...] was born in 1857, and thus, considered chronologically, Gora seems to be almost the same age as his author (born 1861). Both grew up from childhood to adolescence and into youth in the same chronotope of Calcutta in the last decades of the nineteenth century [...] about which he [Tagore] wrote so nostalgically in his [...] autobiography *Jivansmriti*.

In other words, in the sociocultural milieu of the second half of the nineteenth century, the period when the suffering of the ryots described in *Nil Darpan* continued to be relevant, Rabindranath, the novelist, sent Gora to Char Ghoshpur. However, immediately before touching upon indigo planters' oppression, Gora is given a lesson in the vulnerability and divided nature of the peasants and the average Bengali gentleman's indifference to them[30]:

> For the first time in his life, Gora was seeing what our country was like outside the cultured and affluent segments of Kolkata society. How isolated [...]

ignorant and indifferent to its welfare was this vast and isolated rural Bharatvarsha!... What surprised Gora most was that neither Motilal nor Ramapati [educated urban followers of Gora himself] was in the least disturbed by what they saw or heard...

The controversy around Reverend James Long and *Nil Darpan* then is an attempt of the urban, prosperous Bengali intelligentsia to rise above trivial and divisive ideas and to rally behind the ryots, at least culturally, which is proof of the ability of different classes of Indians to fight together against British oppression. However, through Gora's experiences, Rabindranath seemed to present a more usual sight, in terms of division and mutual distrust. The fact that Gora's realization reflects the reality is corroborated by events in Rabindranath's own life when, since 1890, he had had to supervise remote rural parts of the extensive Tagore family estate in Bengal and Orissa[31]:

The Tagore family belonged to the landed aristocracy created by the British raj. This fact, no doubt, coloured the outlook of the young poet and left a lasting mark on his thought-world. The evolution of his thinking is, in many ways, strikingly reminiscent of the hero of his classic novel *Gora*... Like Gora, he went through an excruciating series of experiences, learnt at firsthand how hard it was to help the poor and the oppressed, and to seek justice for them when they lacked self-respect and even a sense of self-interest, when they

betrayed themselves and [...] those who, at grave risks
to themselves, had offered to help them.

The Char Ghoshpur episode in *Gora* is a literary landmark signifying the links of the ryots with the native assistants of British planters and magistrates on the one hand, and members of the genteel Bengali society on the other. Curiously, in the novel, the issue is introduced in a rather oblique way. On a very hot day, Gora and his companion Ramapati are extremely hungry and thirsty when they happen to reach a predominantly Muslim village. The village has one Hindu barber's family, in whose house they can draw water and cook their own food, but the barber has given shelter to a young Muslim boy, son of one Foru Sardar, the local peasants' leader. Therefore, being upper caste Hindus, the gentlemen can't jeopardize their religious identity by eating or drinking there. Feeling baffled and exasperated, they question the barber, and the situation of Char Ghoshpur is revealed. This place, like other zamindari areas, was leased out to British indigo planters[32]:

> ... Char Ghoshpur continued to resist... Foru [...] reduced practically to starvation... This year [...] villagers had managed to raise an early crop of boro paddy on the freshly deposited stretch of river silt. But, the manager of the indigo factory had himself come with a band of lathials and forcibly harvested the grain... Foru Sardar had struck such a hard lathi-blow on the manager's right arm that the saheb had

> [...] that arm amputated. After that incident police oppression [...] had spread [...] like fire.

The arrest of Foru Sardar and many other villagers, the dishonour of the women and the consequent escape of others led to a village of only women and children, with the exception of the Hindu barber who did not have a significant landholding. He had thus given shelter to Foru's son.

Foru's spirited resistance of the indigo planters' oppression was violent, though unpremeditated. For these villagers, it was a question of survival. They were trying to get a crop of paddy harvested before their land and energy got depleted in indigo cultivation. However, even this means of subsistence was snatched away from them. In contrast, Gora is an outsider with no knowledge of the intricacies of the local politics. Yet, he refuses to leave them to their fate. When Gora understands that the alternative to the barber's (presumably defiled) hut is the mansion, three miles away, of Madhob Chatujjye, a Brahmin, the 'tahsildar attached to the indigo factory [...] a regular devil [...] playing host to the daroga [police],'[33] he feels that hospitality from a compatriot who supports the planters and the police so brazenly would be repugnant, and walks back to the barber's hut in the scorching mid-day sun. Gora's decision to stake all for the oppressed people marks the turning point in his career. He confronts the corrupt and cruel Madhob, and the daroga, the brutal police official, directly and openly, accusing them of harming the ryots, which angers the daroga. The tahsildar sends a complaint to the local magistrate Mr Brownlow, who is thus predisposed to consider Gora as a troublemaker. Haranbabu and the young Bengali gentlemen and ladies from Calcutta, in contrast, wait in the local inspection bungalow provided by Mr Brownlow, to recite and perform in front of his distinguished guests and friends, feeling gratified for the invitation: 'There would be a dinner party two days later where the commissioner as well as the lieutenant governor and his wife would be present.'[34] When Gora argues with the magistrate about the white planters' atrocities and miscarriage of justice, the latter hates this forthrightness. Instead, Brownlow appreciates Haranbabu's arguments about the noble spirit of Christianity. It is ironical that Haranbabu not only refuses to recognize Gora, but criticizes him as an upstart in front of the Magistrate himself, and later in the company of the Bengali contingent at the inspection bungalow.

Haranbabu is not Gora's only compatriot to shun him. The Hindu barber of Char Ghoshpur is also afraid, lest Gora's presence leads to further planter and police oppression. Gora's friend Satkori Haldar, an efficient lawyer, also feels that Gora's attempt to get bail for the forty-seven villagers languishing without trial in police lockup would be futile. Racial prejudice translates to punishment for the native subjects, and thus, when the application for bail is submitted by Gora[35]:

> The magistrate took one look at yesterday's intruder [...] and refused the application. Persons ranging in age from a fourteen-year-old boy to an eighty-year-old ancient continued to rot in prison... Satkori said, '... The magistrate suspects that the upper class people have a secret hand in it... Causing injury even to a petty Englishman is like a petty rebellion against the King...'

Still, unlike Haranbabu, Gora could not be a sycophant; he could not remain aloof like the lawyer. He decides to get legal help for the ryots from Calcutta. However, in the meantime, he witnesses a police atrocity and attempts to help a group of students from Calcutta. They were fighting off the local police constables. The policemen abused them when they, unknowingly, took water from a local reserved tank to help an injured friend. This act of resistance gets them arrested. Clearly, even in an emergency, Indians did not have access to the water in their own country. The students, presumably, should have searched for and found out about the rules first and then sought to use the water. After his arrest, Gora refuses to employ a lawyer to defend himself on the ground that 'it is the king's obligation to do justice... But in this kingdom the subjects have to rot in jail because they have no money [...]—I don't want to spend a pie for such justice.'[36] Brownlow sends the students to jail with an order of caning. He definitely remembers Gora's argument on behalf of the ryots of Char Ghoshpur from the previous day and 'sentenced him to one month's rigorous imprisonment... He even claimed that he was being particularly lenient in awarding such a light sentence.'[37]

This may remind the readers of Sashibhushan. Rabindranath was being ironical again. Gora's act of protest and consequently, the imprisonment, provides such a jolt to his friend Binoy and Poreshbabu's daughter Lolita that they spontaneously reject the magistrate's hospitality, Haranbabu's company and the glory of performing before high-ranking British officials, and leave for Calcutta by the next steamer. This proves to be doubly significant as Lolita does not care about a family chaperone and leaves the place, no longer bothered about her maidenly honour and social position. The emergence of the woman in the social sphere had come about earlier in the Brahmo Samaj, which men like Rabindranath and women like Lolita were members of. But the reason of Lolita's gesture turns out to be novel, necessary and pertinent, in Rabindranath's novel. Not violence, but a silent and dignified acceptance of a prison term by Gora inspired his friends' rejection of the material benefits of the British bounty. Their gesture serves as a mark of solidarity for the victims and the protester, who are imprisoned alike. Gora, Binoy and Lolita reiterate a definite political statement, which the peasants led by Foru Sardar and the students had already made. In this context, we may recall Vandana Shiva's pointed reference to the similarities between the simple folks' resistance to indigo cultivation in the past and their resistance towards cash crops in the present. She wrote that the soil and the marginalized human beings have continued to be exploited. However, though once a student of Visva-Bharati, Shiva does not mention either literary activism in general, or Rabindranath's viewpoints in particular, in this context.

Rabindranath's extremely rich and princely grandfather, Dwarkanath Tagore, along with Raja Ram Mohan Roy, were well aware of the triangle formed by zamindars, ryots and indigo planters[38]:

> Rammohun [...] failed to realize the true impact of the system of indigo cultivation on the rural countryside... Dwarkanath Tagore shared this shortcoming [...] [which] becomes even more glaring in view of the fact that the indigo peasants had been agitating against the system for long. Both [...] were themselves planters... The latter even held that the poor classes were better off through the diffusion of purchasing power, which was the result of the introduction of a remunerative cash crop... He observed that [...] the middle classes employed as *sarkar* and in other capacities in the plantations were getting higher salaries...

Is it a coincidence that Rabindranath is strangely and largely silent about his illustrious grandfather? In 'Ryoter Katha,' an essay in *Kalantar*, in 1926, Rabindranath acknowledged that he belonged to a family of zamindars and, therefore, at times, had the interests of this class in his mind. But at the same time, he claimed, it was essential to acknowledge that zamindars had protected the ryots effectively when the indigo planters made attempts to appropriate the poor peasants' landholdings citing non-repayment of loans.[39] He also wrote that the zamindars might possibly have played a benevolent role in the lives of the ryots.

Rabindranath repeatedly tried to help the rural people in such a way that they would eventually become self-reliant, even though in the 1890s, his efforts were thwarted in most cases[40]:

> In my estate, the river was far away and lack of water was a serious problem. I said to my tenants, 'If you dig a well, I shall get it cemented.' They replied, 'You want to fry the fish in the oil of the fish itself! If we dig the well you shall go to heaven through the accumulated virtue of having provided water for the thirsty, while we shall have done the work.' The idea, obviously, was that an account of all such deeds was kept in heaven and while I, having earned great merit, could go to the seventh heaven, the village people would simply get some water. I had to withdraw my proposal... I had built a road from our estate office up to Kushtia. I told the villagers who lived close to the road, 'The upkeep of this road is your responsibility...' It was, in fact, their ox-cart wheels that damaged the road and put it out of use during the rains... They could not bear the thought that others should also enjoy the fruits of their labour. Rather than let that happen, they would put up with inconveniences.

Rabindranath never gave up. He understood that the peasants had lost all faith in themselves. They had simultaneously become self-centred. Suggestions were, therefore, viewed with suspicion. At the same time, he commiserated with them. Therefore, in order to implement plans that would sustain both the land and the people and keep them united, in terms of cooperation, he continued his efforts, sometimes failing, and sometimes achieving success[41]:.

> First hand experiences about the hardships faced during famines and natural calamities prompted the poet to suggest arrangement of co-operative grain stores (*dharmagolas*). After the harvest, each ryot was to contribute a part of his crop to build up a stock of the *dharmagola*. The grain thus stored would help them to tide over lean periods. The ryot would also be advanced seeds at nominal rates.

Rabindranath understood that the rural population had to pay exorbitant rates of interest to moneylenders to get seeds, for other important aspects related to farming, to pay rent or for their day-to-day survival if crops failed, and they could not repay the accumulating amount. This burden would crush them and the mortgaged land and belongings would be gone, leaving them paupers[42]:

> This actually led him to open a cooperative bank, Kaligram Krishi Bank, at Patisar in 1905 for group-based small loans to rural farmers... The cooperative

societies that Tagore organized worked simultaneously with the Krishi Bank. He set up these societies so that the villagers could unite to eradicate poverty, ill-health and illiteracy... Muhammad Yunus of Bangladesh won the Nobel Peace Prize in 2006 along with his Grameen Bank, for their efforts through micro credit to create economic and social development from below... He admitted that he had been inspired by the ideals and techniques adopted by Rabindranath at the turn of the twentieth century in this respect... Rabindranath started the bank with borrowed capital for which he had to pay an interest of 8 per cent. Later, even a major portion of the Nobel Prize money was ploughed into it... in actuality, the peasants paid 6 per cent interest... When the bank collapsed after remaining in operation for thirty years, the poet lost much of his invested money.

He sent his son Rathindranath, not to Oxford or Cambridge or Harvard, but to Illinois to study agricultural science. Rathindranath wrote[43]:

Towards the end of 1909 I returned home... I settled down at Shelidah and led the life of a country gentleman. A farm was laid out, seeds of maize, clover and alfalfa were imported from America; discs, harrows, and such modern implements suitable to Indian conditions were introduced. Even a small laboratory was fitted up for soil testing.

Rabindranath spent whatever was required to enable the farmers to lead a proper life and reduce both their dependence and the burden on the land. In the process, he introduced the idea of the pooling of land for the use of tractors. In order to solve the problem of the surplus agricultural labour for the major part of the year, he encouraged them—at great cost to himself—to produce suitable fruits and vegetables during different seasons, so that they would not have to depend on the crop of paddy only and the land would be used properly. His expensive and time-consuming experiment with Nainital potatoes and earlier, the breeding of silkworms, had failed. Undeterred, he continued to work relentlessly for their welfare[44]:

> He persuaded the peasants in his estate at Potisar to organize themselves into a welfare community which came to be known as Hitaishi Sabha, covering about 125 villages with sixty to seventy thousand inhabitants. The Sabha raised its own funds, to which the Tagore estate contributed, maintained schools, hospitals and other centres of common welfare and was self-governing in its constitution.

In *Ghare Baire* (1916), we find Nikhil, the zamindar, being misunderstood and called a traitor to the cause of India's freedom struggle when he refused to burn foreign clothes in the name of the swadeshi movement. But it is Nikhil who had already borne enormous losses quietly by procuring, attempting to sell, and having to buy the whole lot of

Indian cotton back, in the absence of buyers among the poor villagers. He was reviled and compared with other zamindars who had given permission to burn foreign clothes. His effigy was burnt. In the volatile political atmosphere of the country, zamindars were divided into two categories, in public perception: those accepting swadeshi were in the first category and proclaimed as heroes, but if one opposed thoughtless destruction to safeguard the interests of the poor rural population, he would be condemned as a traitor. Any zamindar like Nikhil, who continued to work quietly for his compatriots, could easily be labelled a sycophant, and his silent personal sacrifices could be erased from public memory. Why did Rabindranath think of portraying the failed attempts of Nikhil for the villagers with such care, just as he had written about Sashibhushan and Gora earlier? His own experience was that the attempts to sustain the village land, economy and people were often faced with resistance.

The kind of work Rabindranath tried to do was not only for the sustenance of the soil and to optimize its use, but also to improve its condition at great personal cost. Though he was consistently suspected and thwarted by the rural people, he continued to make personal sacrifices for their resuscitation. He refused to be the coercive, authoritarian zamindar who would have been obeyed out of fear anyway. Nor would he permit the upper class intelligentsia to dictate measures that would not benefit the peasants. Rabindranath continued to grapple with the socio-economic conventions and expectations of the upper class society he belonged to by birth, and made attempts to stand—if necessary, alone—not only with, but for, the land and its people, as his vocation. He understood the nature of the storm raging around him and continued to face it alone with utmost courage and conviction. Where, possibly, did he get the strength to overcome personal loss and continue to work against such odds?

NOTES

1. Pal, *Rabijibani* Volume II, 233; my translation.
2. Ibid., 234. We appreciate Daniel Hamilton's work with villagers in the Sunderbans but do not generally remember Rabindranath in this context.
3. I have used the word ryot throughout this chapter to signify, interchangeably, Indian peasants compelled to grow indigo, and the sections of people specified by Nandi Bhatia in *Acts of Authority/ Acts of Resistance*:

   According to the introduction in Mitra, *Nil Darpan*, lxxvi, for the British officials the term *ryot*, as C Anderson and Boyle defined it in 1881, meant 'the immediate occupant of the soil, whether he be considered as proprietor or tenant. The word, in its most extensive signification means a subject; but it is usually applied to the numerous and inferior class of people, who hold and cultivate small plots of land on their own account.' (134)

   See Nandi Bhatia, *Acts of Authority/ Acts of Resistance: Theater and Politics in Colonial and Postcolonial India* Ann Arbor: University of Michigan Press, 2004.

Technically, though, there were different classes of cultivators since 1859. We learn from Bipasha Raha's *The Plough and the Pen*, 73–74 that the government enacted Act X in 1859... Ryots were classified into three groups: ryots holding at fixed rates, occupancy ryots and non-occupancy ryots. Ryots holding land at a rate unchanged for twenty years before the date of rent-suits brought against them by zamindars belonged to the first group. Zamindars could not enhance their rent... Any ryot who had cultivated or held lands for a period of 12 years was an occupancy ryot, as long as he paid rent... Ryots without the right of occupancy were not protected by the law.

4. Tagore, *Chhinnapatravali*, 157; my translation.
5. Quoted by Bipasha Raha, 'Rabindranath Tagore; Attempt at Revival of Villages,' 180.
6. Rathindranath Tagore, *On the Edges of Time*, 28.
7. Alam and Chakravarty, *Essential Tagore*, 55.
8. Tagore, *Chithipatra* Volume V, 150–151; my translation.
9. Ibid., 160–161; my translation.
10. Kripalani, *Tagore: Biography*, 144–145.
11. Rabindranath Tagore, 'The Postmaster' tr. Debendranath Mitter in *Mashi and Other Stories.* (1918) (Delhi: Macmillan, 2001) 161. For another version of discussion of these three short stories in the context of *Glimpses of Bengal* see Debarati Bandyopadhyay, 'Viewing the Margins: Rabindranath Tagore's *Chhinnapatra* (Glimpses of Bengal) and Stories in *Rabindranath Tagore: A Concourse (Assays in Art, Literature and Translation)* ed. Debarati Bandyopadhyay (Kolkata: Business Economics Publications, 2017) 13–26.
12. Ibid., 161.

13. Ibid., 167.
14. Tagore, 'The Child's Return,' 47.
15. Ibid., 48.
16. Tagore, 'Cloud and Sun,' 43–44.
17. Ibid., 44.
18. Ibid., 45–46.
19. Ibid., 46.
20. Ibid., 48.
21. Tagore, 'Civilization and Progress,' 80.
22. M.N. MacDonald, 'Indigo planting in India,' 387.
23. Ibid., 387.
24. Ibid., 391–92.
25. Ibid., 389.
26. Shiva, 'Ecology, Equity and Self-reliance,' 85–86.
27. Spangenberg, Review of *The Blue Mutiny: The Indigo Disturbances in Bengal 1859–1862*, 167–68.
28. Sukumar Sen, *History of Bengali Literature*, 183.
29. Ray and Kundu, '*Gora*: A Critical Introduction,' xi.
30. Rabindranath Tagore, *Gora*, tr. Sujit Mukherjee 170–171.
31. Sudhir Sen, 'Tagore's Ideas,' 23.
32. Tagore, *Gora*, tr. Sujit Mukherjee 172.
33. Ibid., 173.
34. Ibid., 178–9.
35. Ibid., 182–3.
36. Ibid.,184.
37. Ibid., 188.
38. Raha, *The Plough and the Pen*, 52.
39. Tagore, 'Ryoter Katha,' 655.

40. Tagore, *My Life in My Words*, 109.
41. Raha, *Living a Dream: Rabindranath Tagore and Rural Resuscitation*, 131.
42. Ibid., 130–1.
43. Rathindranath Tagore, *On the Edges of Time*, 73–74.
44. Kripalani, *Tagore: Biography*, 164.

Chapter 2

The Calm: Ecophilosophy in *Gitanjali* and Beyond

Rabindranath's dilemma regarding the twin desires of his mind gradually became important. A part of him found it intolerable that a section of the human society would oppress the other and exploit nature selfishly. There was another part in him that remembered the lessons of the Upanishads and sought peace and harmony in all existence. Rabindranath felt that the worldview in India is non-aggressive or non-violent in the most comprehensive sense as it suggests peace not only between nations and races but also in the relationships working across species and encompassing all existence. It harmonizes the living and the non-living, the human and the nonhuman. The genesis of this consciousness, in relation to the Vedas and the Upanishads, is to be found in young Rabi's training by his father, Maharshi Debendranath Tagore[1]:

> In the winter of 1872–73 when Rabi was eleven
> years and nine months old, the Maharshi personally
> presided over the investiture of the sacred thread of
> [...] Rabindra... the gayatri which they were made
> to recite left a deep impression on Rabi's mind. The
> splendid cadence and intonation of this Vedic verse
> appealed strongly to his feeling for rhythm and his
> sense of the mysterious sublime. The gayatri remained
> his lifelong companion and he continued to find in it
> a source of contemplative insight and strength long
> after he had discarded the sacred thread.

From the moment of the investiture of the sacred thread—the mark of becoming a Brahmin—the boy was entitled to recite the gayatri mantra regularly with its invocation to Earth, Firmament and Heaven. Even without understanding the full importance of Vedic philosophy, it became possible for young Rabi, with his boyish enthusiasm, to be initiated into the world of ideas that took him beyond the mundane concerns, selfish thoughts and immediate necessities. The mantra inspired him to contemplate the vast expanses of the earth, sky and what lay beyond.

Soon after the initiation into the beauty and order of greater existence, young Rabi had the opportunity to travel with his father to the western Himalayas. The boy learnt about the green rural world as if through a series of pictures viewed through the window of the train. The train itself suggests, on the one hand, both the progress and the spread of British control and technology throughout India, and on the other, the means of the destruction of stretches of land, as well as of pollution. Maharshi Debendranath took him first to Bolpur and later to Amritsar. With the gayatri mantra ringing in his ears, he travelled from the eastern part of India to the northern part of it.

Accompanying the Maharshi, singing hymns in the Golden Temple, which is sacred to Sikhs, while passing through Amritsar, and learning to pay homage to other religions, young Rabi imbibed ideals that expanded the horizons of his mind. But his real acquaintance with Sanskrit and the Upanishads came in the lap of the Himalayas[2]:

> By the time father and son reached the foot of the Himalayas, it was April, the beginning of summer in the plains and of spring in the mountains. Their destination was Dalhousie [...] over 7,000 ft. above the sea. The mountain sides were covered with tall, graceful deodars and a riot of spring flowers which the boy had never seen before and of which the names were still unknown to him. High up were the snow peaks and beneath, as the road turned and wound upwards, he saw great gorges with thick clusters of giant trees, underneath whose shade a little rivulet trickled down, 'like a little daughter of the hermitage playing at the feet of hoary sages wrapt in meditation.' Already the spirit of Kalidasa was stirring in the eleven-year, wonder-eyed boy.

> At last they reached their cottage at Bakrota, perched on the top of a mountain. The boy was now free to wander about and feast his eyes on the loveliness and grandeur of the Himalayas spread out before him... The Maharshi [...] was a stern disciplinarian and taskmaster... long before the sun rose, he woke up the boy and practised with him Sanskrit declensions... The Maharshi would then chant verses from the Upanishads, the boy listening, spellbound by the sonorous rhythm.

But in learning about the Vedas and Upanishads from his father, what would young Rabi actually get to know about nature and God? Would this knowledge tell him how these were interrelated? Was this wisdom in circulation among those Indians who knew the Vedas, the Upanishads and the Sanskrit classics, during the period in which Tagore was born? He realized that his father was the leader of the Brahmo Samaj, the monotheistic religious movement that was based strictly upon the precepts found in the Upanishads. But, what did the Vedas and Upanishads say about the nature of the universe and the relation between the living and the non-living in this world? Did these ancient Indian books talk about ecological harmony? It is essential to answer these questions before Rabindranath's experience of the Vedas and Upanishads can be appreciated in the larger context of his life and work.

The ancient idea that the many gods in Hinduism are

actually manifestations of the one God tells us of the concept of a Supreme Power creating, giving life to, and thereby unifying, all that exists in the universe. This concept serves as one explanation of the ecological harmony envisaged by the Vedic seers[3]:

> The earliest Sanskrit texts, the Vedas and Upanishads, have almost exclusively accepted and preached about the non-dualism of the supreme power that existed before the creation. God as the efficient cause, and nature (Prakriti) as the material cause of the universe is unconditionally accepted as is their harmonious relationship.

In this idea of the Creator and creation, the One Supreme Existence has different names, depending upon the areas of nature that are being presided over or nurtured at that moment[4]:

> He is one, but the wise call him by different names; such as Indra, Mitra, Varuna, Agni, Divya—one who pervades all the luminous bodies, the source of light, Suparna—the protector and preserver of the universe; whose works are perfect; Matriswa—powerful like wind; Garutman—mighty by nature.

In Hinduism, therefore, all that exists in nature is made by one supreme God. It is for this reason that 'one finds [...] "Visvakarman" in the Sanskrit text, meaning "all-maker" of the universe'[5]. A simple equation emerges from this reading:

there is one God—the creator—and the whole creation with multifarious levels of existence, comes from this Supreme Power. Therefore, the 'very idea of environment as an objective entity is beyond comprehension for a Vedic ṛṣi (seer)... Whatever is in the microcosms (Pinda) is projected in the larger and bigger cosmos (the Brahmand), and conversely, the world around is present in the body within'[6]. It is in this sense of human existence as an integral part of general existence in the world that the Vedic seers had described life and environment—human and nonhuman living beings, and inert things—as belonging and existing together.

In ancient Hindu philosophy it was thought[7]:

Nothing exists which is not a part of everyone's existence. The distinction between Man as the enjoyer and fruits of the Earth as the material for enjoyment is conspicuous by its absence... The concern for environment, therefore, starts from the other end. The present-day concern of the modern West-oriented man starts with the assumption that we have to take care of the environment as it affects our living. On the other hand, the ancient Indian seer's or poet's (the Seer and the Poet were one) concern started with the assumption that we are a part of a larger existence, in order to become the whole, or, in other words, in order to live a full life, we have to offer ourselves to the Universal or to whole or full existence... The

> fullness of life is visualized [...] through the kinship image, the earth as the mother, the sky as the father, the vegetation as brother or sister.

The living and the inanimate combine in nature to form a whole, and this relationship is usually expressed in terms of a thread running through all, or a stream without a beginning or an end. Each image of this type reflects the idea of ecological coherence and harmony.

In the world of the Vedas and Upanishads, Man had the knowledge that the individual or the species is a part of the larger whole and it is only in the context of this existence that human life gains its meaning. Hence, the non-living components of the world, like water and sunlight, would be considered as givers and their gifts were not only gratefully acknowledged but also prayed for. There are various expressions of ecological unity in the Vedas. The Rig Veda (I/164/42) says that an integral relationship exists between life and water: 'Waters rule over the world of Vegetation, they are the sustainers of all that moves; we beg of them nourishment.'[8] In the Rig Veda (X/190/2) the sun is praised for its power: 'The sun releases all forms from the captivity of their shapelessness; he is truly a poet.'[9] The idea was that the cosmic and earthly powers continued to nourish life. It was a basic human responsibility, therefore, to express gratitude towards these benevolent powers. It was also necessary that each human being with this knowledge should continue to enshrine and worship these values that sustained life[10]:

> There are different ends in life regarded as debts which one is obliged to pay. Thus with sacrifices, a man pleases the gods, with Vedic studies, the sages (ṛṣis), with children, the fathers, and with food and shelter, man... We notice the concept of continuity that is the invisible common thread running through these; continuity of sacrifices, of Vedic studies, raising a family and kindness to men are factors which assure continuity of the spiritual and physical well-being of society.

A continuous repayment of a debt of gratitude to nature ensures harmony in existence. In this way, the earth, endowed with the benevolence of the sun and impregnated by the rain, becomes the saviour of the creatures as the mother. Therefore, a hymn in the Atharva Veda (XII/42) expresses this gratitude felt towards the soil or the Earth-mother[11]:

> 'You who nurture the five kinds of crops
> And are cause for their grains to swell
> Out to ripeness.
> O Earth, wife to the lavish cloud,
> It's, to you, to your open-hand, that
> I [bow].'

To the Vedic seer, the birds, the winds, the dust particles, the trees sometimes stirring and sometimes remaining calm, the flame of the fire, both fertile and barren or rocky land, the forest and the expanses of water—all come to mean the totality of existence.[12] It is in this wholeness of creation that human existence becomes consequential. The Taittiriya Upanishad (2.6) reveals the relationship between the Creator and the creation and the concept of their unity is evoked: 'He (the Atman) desired: I will become many, will propagate myself. Accordingly he practiced self-mortification. After that he created the entire Universe, whatever exists. After having created it, he entered into it.'[13] The Isa Upanishad (1) highlights the idea of an 'overall unified view of creation in Upanishads' as[14]:

> By the Lord enveloped must this all be,
> Whatever moving thing there is in the
> moving world.

We also find a reflection of the integral relationship between the Creator and all that exists in creation in the Moksaparva of the *Mahabharata*[15]:

> Yudhistir asked Bhisma Pitamaha—How was the world created? What was the position of creatures at the time of Pralaya? Who is the maker of the sea, sky, mountain, clouds, fire (Agni), air and other things in the world? How are all creatures made, how cleanliness and impurity emerged, and how Dharma (religion) and Adharma came into existence. In reply Bhisma said—God is the form of Sṛṣṭi. He created the Purusa out of [the] one-thousandth part of his body...

Maharshi Veda Vyas, considered as the poet of the *Mahabharata*, thus states the belief that God and nature (Prakriti) were the one and the same. This viewpoint is relevant, as it reiterates the philosophy of the Vedas and Upanishads and also strengthens the idea that since different parts of the world/creation are parts of the manifestation of God, everything in the world is related to everybody and everything else[16]:

> The Father of all creatures, God, made the sky. From it he made water and from water he made fire (Agni) and air (Vayu). From fire and air, Prithvi (earth) came into existence. Mountains are his bones, Earth is the flesh, Sea is the blood, Sky is his abdomen, Air is his breath, Agni is his Teja, rivers are his nerves. The sun and moon, which are called Agni and Soma, are the eyes of Brahman. The upper part of the sky is his head, Prithvi (earth) is his feet and the directions (Disha) are his hands.

As in all creation myths, here too, the inanimate world is lovingly created at the beginning when there is still no mention of human beings. The display of human arrogance in considering human intelligence and the capacity to control and destroy, at will, everything else in the world, is conspicuously irrelevant to such a worldview.

The *Bhagavad Gita* is considered by many Hindus as the most philosophical part of ancient knowledge. In the *Bhagavad Gita*, Lord Krishna tells Arjuna: 'Of all that is material and all that is spiritual in this world, know for certain that I am both its origin and dissolution.'[17] From creation to complete annihilation, the cosmos remains one entity and that entity is a manifestation of the supreme will of the Creator. The significance of this statement in the *Bhagavad Gita* has great relevance to our discussion, not only because it serves to remind us that faith in the omnipotence of the Creator can only mean that human beings have no special position in the cosmos or creation, but also because Rabindranath had indicated the nature of his careful reading of the *Bhagavad Gita* in *Journey to Persia and Iraq: 1932*. Travelling in an airplane to Bushire, Persia, Rabindranath wrote how the teachings of the *Bhagavad Gita* can be completely overturned if the lives of unsuspecting human beings and other living beings are destroyed by means of weapons dropped by these planes during the time of war (anticipating vividly the carnage of Hiroshima and Nagasaki, something that he was fortunately no longer alive to witness)[18]:

> Herald of the modern age, the flying machine is not susceptible to sentiment, it has no use for beauty, it elbows aside whatever does not serve its purpose... As it rises higher and higher, it reduces the play of our own senses to that of one alone—of sight—and even that is not left in its fullness. All the signs for which we believe the earth to be obviously and variously real, are gradually wiped out, resolving its three-dimensional picture into lines of one dimension only. Thus deprived

of its substantiality, its hold on our mind and heart is loosened. And it is borne in on me how terrible such aloofness can become, once it is found expedient to rain destruction on the vagueness below. Who is the slayer, who the slain? Who is kin, who is stranger? It is a travesty of this teaching of the Gita that the flying machine has raised on high.

Rabindranath appreciated the sheer 'superior skill', 'indomitable perseverance' and 'unflagging courage' of the Western people, the inventors of the airplane, 'a different race' from the ancient Indian mythical users of the 'air chariot', like Indra and, on invitation, 'mortals like King Dushyanta.'[19] But he simultaneously criticized the Western arrogance and indifference to the plight of both the earth and the beings nestling in her lap in dropping bombs, the harbingers of annihilation. In the *Bhagavad Gita*, the powers of creation and annihilation lie in the hands of a Supreme Power who is beyond ordinary human comprehension, and in causing a rain of bombs from the airplane, the terrestrial political powers seem to have ironically appropriated the role of God. Rabindranath's observation on the use of airplanes for heinous offences against all existence—in terms of what Krishna is supposed to have taught Arjuna on the battlefield of Kurukshetra—reminds us that the great warrior must repose his faith in God as the final arbiter of right and wrong, justice and injustice, and life and death, and raise his mind beyond the mundane, illusory bonds of kinship and friendship. This is proclaimed not to erase the bonds that make human life meaningful on earth, but to assure Arjuna that both the slayer and the slain are one, as they both lie within God. Rabindranath perceived that the rich philosophical understanding of life, enshrined in the *Bhagavad Gita*, has been given a morbid twist in authoring such suicidal destruction.

The lessons from the ancient Sanskrit scriptures provided Rabindranath with a comprehension of the nature of life, death and the earth. This knowledge prompted him to read literary texts in a way ecocritics would most appreciate. Certain significant texts of ancient Sanskrit literature serve as a rich source of an aesthetic expression of the idea of a harmony existing between nature and human existence. Rabindranath consciously compared Kalidasa's Shakuntala with Shakespeare's Miranda from *The Tempest*. He commented on the two young girls' relationship with their surroundings quite extensively.

In his texts, Kalidasa describes ancient Indian ideas about nature, through the sacrosanct environs in and around a hermitage in a forest[20]:

> The hermitage is the place which radiates confidence in sentient and non-sentient beings, and which makes animals, birds, trees, coparceners of man. Young trees are watered in the evening by young virgins, who move apart from the watered trees so that the birds may feel free to drink in the tree beds. Young deer block

> the passage for the housewives of forester seers, as if they were their own children demanding as a matter of right their share of the wild rice brought by them. Kalidasa in his *Raghuvamsa* has depicted the scene with great reverence...

Time and again the hermitage motif is brought into play in Sanskrit drama as a measure of serenity, purity and radiance of the All-being and is a countercheck against the impurity, hypocrisy and crookedness of court life.

It is for this reason that the King Dushyanta's attempt to kill a deer in the vicinity of the hermitage draws a timely warning from the ascetics of the place, in Kalidasa's *Shakuntala*. Not only is bloodshed prohibited in such a place but each plant and animal is shown as an integral part of life in the hermitage. Shakuntala, Anasuya and Priyamvada know spontaneously that they are the surrogate mothers of the young deer and trees. It is the depiction of this harmonious ecological relationship that made Kalidasa's work so valuable to Rabindranath.

Rabindranath wrote the long essay 'Shakuntala' in 1902 for *Bangadarshan*, one of the most highly reputed literary magazines in Bengali.[21] Comparing Shakuntala with Shakespeare's Miranda, he wrote about Shakespeare's heroine that she has 'no intimate relationship with nature on that island... Shakuntala [...] is one with the forest'.[22] The vital relationship between Shakuntala and her environment draws the highest praise from Rabindranath. This is probably because he found in it a revelation of the most poignant expression possible in literature—of human love for, and life in, nature[23]:

> Her heart's creeper binds everything, animate and inanimate, with grateful tendrils of love... Of all the literature in the world, only the fourth act of *Shakuntala* shows us how grievous and heart-rending the parting between a human being and a forest can be... I think no country other than India could have brought about this sense of implicit union between dissimilars.

Rabindranath read Kalidasa's *Shakuntala*, section by section here. In terms of a fine sensitivity towards ecology, this reading of the ancient Sanskrit text prompted him to claim for it a unique position in world literature. It is precisely this ecological harmony that Rabindranath found lacking in *The Tempest*. Rabindranath appears to have felt that there could have been an establishment of ecological harmony or, at least, a gentle relationship among Prospero, Miranda and nature on the island in *The Tempest*, and that this never came to be in Shakespeare's worldview: '... external nature takes on human shape in [...] Ariel... In *The Tempest*, oppression, rule, rigour... nature assumes the shape of man yet is not bound to him by the heart's ties; in *Shakuntala*, trees, birds, and beasts retain their own shape yet unite with man.'[24]

Shakuntala begins with the Sage's disciple calling out to King Dushyanta, the hunter, that he should not kill the deer, as the ashrama offers refuge to all; it then moves on to show the affection, of the young girls of the forest hermitage, towards the various animals and plants; and finally shows the protagonist finding it difficult to bid farewell to her foster family and friends, both human and nonhuman. As a literary critic, Rabindranath highlighted how each and every one of these instances revealed the true value of individual human life as extant only in its relation to the collective and the natural, in terms of love as well as harmonious living.

When Sage Kanva's foster daughter was moving away from the forest hermitage for her husband Dushyanta's palace, there was a poignant scene of mutual sorrow in which the birds and animals suffer as much as the human protagonist herself[25]:

> The grass drops from the deer's jaws,
> The peacocks dance no more,
> And every creeper sheds its leaves
> As if tears did flow.

In order to emphasize the characteristics of the bond that existed between Shakuntala and her nonhuman loved ones, Rabindranath chose Kalidasa's depiction of a touching moment when Shakuntala was leaving the forest hermitage and, feeling a tug from behind, asked who was pulling her. Her foster father Kanva then answered[26]:

> ... He whose jaws, when chafed by kusha grass,
> With oil of ingudi you would smear...
> ...your son, that baby deer.

The deer's gesture reveals that Shakuntala has been a mother to it for some time now, taking care that its tender mouth wouldn't be hurt by the sharp edges of grass, even though, biologically, she would give birth to her son Bharata, a few months later. Rabindranath wrote: 'The external nature that Kalidasa describes [...] does not remain external [...] through Shakuntala's being.'[27]

In contrast to Shakuntala's 'maternal' instinct towards even the nonhuman in her habitat, we have Rabindranath's reference to the same expression in the context of Miranda, on the verge of leaving the island on which she grew up, but this serves only to highlight the absence of any ecological bond in Shakespeare's play: 'If [...] plucked from that maternal soil where she has lived since infancy, it would not cause any wrench to her being.'[28] It is highly significant that in Rabindranath's positive reception of Kalidasa's work, there is a reminder of the essential relation that ought to regulate the lives of human beings and their nonhuman neighbours, friends and, in the case of a person like Shakuntala, even family. It is doubly significant that Rabindranath highlighted the fact that it was not Shakuntala who, in a monologue, soliloquy or forlorn speech, had expressed her love for the trees and animals; rather, as a part of his benedictory speech, it is Kanva who describes the nature of the bond they mutually share, addressing them and placing the individual firmly among the many mute parts of the creation. Their silent presence forms an integral part of the wholeness of the forest hermitage[29]:

> 'O assembled trees of the hermitage,
> She who has never quenched her thirst
> Had she not watered you first...
> All of you, bid her farewell.'

Rabindranath criticized *The Tempest* for revealing a limitation at the level of ecological thought. He seems to have felt that the love that brought the human, other sentient creatures, and the very place together in *Shakuntala*, was completely eclipsed by human rapacity in Shakespeare's play: 'In *The Tempest*, man has not enlarged his being [...] beneficently in a tie of love... *The Tempest* is in content as it is in name: a conflict between nature and humankind.'[30]

To Rabindranath, the ideal situation would have been one of amity in ecological relations. The degrees of deviation from it are marks of indiscipline and a utilitarian attitude in human beings: 'Intractable human nature raises such tempests.'[31] It is not as if Rabindranath praised Kalidasa's world and condemned the worldview presented in *The Tempest* indiscriminately[32]:

> His [Tagore's] reading of Kalidas was influenced by his deep involvement with ancient Indian ideals as interpreted by the nineteenth-century Brahmo Samaj, to which he belonged... His understanding of the texts is guided not solely by literary merit nor by aesthetic criteria, but by the value systems implicit in the texts... Rabindranath is not as euphoric over Shakespeare as are many of his compatriots, including Bankimchandra

and Shri [...] Aurobindo [...] who found Sanskrit
drama wanting in power to represent the complex
problems of life in comparison to the Shakespearean
or the Greek. Rabindranath's differing view is not due
to parochialism of taste and certainly not any cultural
chauvinism. It is chiefly because of his understanding
of the relation between humankind and nature and the
place of violence and peace, power and contentment
in human society and the cosmic order.

Realistically speaking, there cannot be complete ecological harmony in a world where human beings predominate. This remains the ideal to aspire to, though. There are wide-ranging problems plaguing and marring a perfect ecological harmony, and literature reflects this condition. Therefore, Rabindranath's explanation of the beginning of the fifth act of *Shakuntala* shows that just as Dushyanta had once made an attempt to destroy an animal's life in Kanva's forest hermitage, so also in the palace, there is persecution of Shakuntala herself. To Rabindranath, Dushyanta's fluctuating interest in various women, coupled with Durvasa's curse, make the rejection of a pregnant Shakuntala in the royal court, complete. The way in which he describes the plight of Shakuntala reveals his respect and yearning for the ideal of ecological sustenance and the harmony that is found in the music of life. On being rejected, she gazes like a doe struck by an arrow that a trusted hand sends to her and the 'music playing through the first four acts is stilled in an instant.'[33]

Rabindranath felt that Kalidasa was right in not sending back Shakuntala to Kanva's hermitage as 'her relation with the universe has changed' and it would therefore be a 'cruel and grotesque incongruity to re-establish her among her old relationships.'[34] The trauma of rejection all around places the individual in a precarious situation. The aura of ingenuousness and simple faith in the world as it has always appeared to be, undergo a crucial and life-changing re-examination. With experience tempering innocent faith the hard way, an old refuge must be given up before a new sanctuary can be conscientiously created: 'The easy-won heaven is thus easily despoilt; [...] the heaven of dedicated labour... won through repentance and meditation... is eternal.'[35] Rabindranath's reference to the 'first paradise' as beautiful yet vulnerable, reminds us of the instantaneous attraction and love between Dushyanta and Shakuntala. It is only when long, patient years of separation, repentance, silent adoration and veneration have taught the worth of true love to the philanderer king that the lovers can be united permanently. There is reciprocation of commitment. In the case of human beings' relationship with nature, the initial easy appreciation of beauty and serenity is, similarly, transitory. In the context of the eternal terrestrial drama, living at a place, loving it and labouring wholeheartedly to guarantee its sustenance can ensure the survival of that cherished world. Rabindranath, as a literary critic, a poet inspired by this understanding of the world, a boy who grew up learning about the Upanishads and the man who created the concept of ecologically harmonious life and education in Santiniketan-Sriniketan, was well aware of the forces that threatened that treasured existence and the urgency with which it merited vigilant cultivation[36]:

> ...[W]hat appears most interesting is Rabindranath's privileging of one kind of poetry: his criticism had a specific function in respect of his own creative activities. Perhaps that was not unexpected in the case of a critic who was also a poet. His criticism was at the same time an apologia for his own poetry.

An effort to explore the possibility of existence of a spontaneous utterance, as inspired by the Upanishads and Sanskrit classics, of an ecophilosophical perception in Rabindranath's work requires us to turn to *Gitanjali*. The history of the publication and reception of *Gitanjali*'s English translation, at the end of 1912, becomes important in this context. In the beginning, Rabindranath loved nature as a beautiful presence. He paid homage to that beauty in poem after poem in his youth. But this romantic effusion gradually led to the germination of a deeper nature-consciousness. One end of a broad spectrum of ecocritical practices 'shades off into a neo-Romantic spiritualism that [...] asserts the healing power of living in the countryside or vicariously enjoying it through literature about rural idylls.'[37] In this sense, the events of the year 1910 become important in our discussion of Rabindranath.

On the eve of a proposed journey to England at the period, he fell ill and had to go to Shelidah, to recuperate. At this point, Rabindranath's attempt to present his poems to the culturally different audience in England becomes inextricably bound to the expression of his writing about nature. We read in his letter[38]:

> It was then the month of Chaitra (March–April), the air was thick with the fragrance of mango-blossoms and all hours of the day were delirious with the song of birds. When a child is full of vigour, he does not think of his mother. It is only when he is tired that he needs to nestle in her lap. That was exactly my position. With all my heart and with all my holiday I seemed to have settled comfortably in the arms of Chaitra, without missing a particle of light, its air, its scene and its song… It is an odd habit of mine […] that when the air strikes my bones they tend to respond in music. Yet I had not the energy to write anything new. So I took up the poems of Gitanjali and set myself to translate them one by one… I simply felt an urge to recapture through the medium of another language the feelings and sentiments which had created such a feast of joy within me in the days gone by…

The lover of the beauty of nature turned into the essential human being trying to find solace and succour in nature, viewed as the mother. In the poems of *Gitanjali*, we find a sustained expression of Rabindranath's nature-philosophy, in terms akin to that of the idea of pantheism enshrined in the Vedas and the Upanishads. In poem 69 of *Gitanjali*, Rabindranath writes[39]:

> The same stream of life that runs through my veins night and day runs through the world and dances in rhythmic measures.
>
> It is the same life that shoots in joy through the dust of the earth in numberless blades of grass and breaks into tumultuous waves of leaves and flowers.
>
> It is the same life that is rocked in the ocean-cradle of birth and of death, in ebb and flow.
>
> I feel my limbs are made glorious by the touch of this world of life. And my pride is from the life-throb of ages dancing in my blood this moment.

The poet and the universe feel the same rhythm and joy of Creation. This poem represents the supreme expression of the essential unity of man, nature and God[40]:

> Rabindranath does not accept literature as imitation of the external world. But he does not deny that the world is the cause of literature. In *The Religion of Man*, he writes that art is the response of the creative human soul to the call of the real. It is not an imitation of external reality but a response to that reality. He refers to a verse in the Atharva Veda where the world has been described as the poem of God, 'devasya kavyam'. The ancients used to call the poet 'prajapati', creator,

and his creation another world, fictional but based on
the fundamental rules of nature.

In the poem from *Gitanjali*, the joy of life, which forms the foundation of every particle in existence, including individual human consciousness, repeatedly reminds us of the message of the Upanishads. This joy inspires the expression of human emotions in art[41]:

> The whole purpose of human creation, like God's, is *ananda* (joy). The Upanishads, says Rabindranath, never tire of talking of *anandarupamamritam yadvibhati* [the being that shines forth in joyous and immortal form]. From a speck of dust to the stars in the heavens, everything is the manifestation of truth and beauty, joy and immortality... Like joy, it [beauty] is not a matter of sensory pleasure, since beauty in art includes the unpleasant, the ugly, the painful, the distorted as well as what is conventionally considered lovely. Here Rabindranath is clearly in agreement with the theory of rasa which stipulates the transformation of the bhavas, the mundane emotions (which are universal), into rasa or aesthetic joy, the ultimate delight produced by literature.

In *Gitanjali* (poem 69), the poet describes a sense as well the rapture of being at one with nature, artistically. This nature is a multifarious, colourful and glorious expression of the divine act of Creation and is represented in poetic art in such a way that we tend to move out of the sphere of our individual interest to enter, with delight (reminding us of that aspect of the divine that signifies rasa), into the world of love for all things and beings in nature. Following the Upanishads, Rabindranath sought the Supreme Being in nature, in a manifestation of a pantheistic sentiment. As a result, nature is supremely important, in itself, to him. We have learnt from Deep Ecology in the latter half of the twentieth century that nature should be valued for its own sake and not for exploiting potential natural resources necessary to sustain human civilization. Though Rabindranath was writing about these ideas in 1910, there seems to be a similarity between him and the Deep Ecologists regarding their views about nature. In other words, a forest is not to be viewed as a potential source of fuel and timber, nor is a river to be viewed, for instance, only as a source of electricity, but rather each is to be viewed for being as it is, as much a part of earth as man.

It emerges as a basic idea among all great eco-conscious thinkers and philosophers that nature has a right to exist by or in itself. In poem 48 of *Gitanjali*, Rabindranath denounces the attitude of those who do not recognize the intrinsic worth of nature and natural beauty for their own sake: 'The morning sea of silence broke into ripples of bird songs; and the flowers were all merry by the roadside; and the wealth of gold was scattered through the rift of the clouds while we busily went on our way and paid no heed'[42]. In the poem, it is only the narrator who expresses a wish to seek repose in nature while his companions, being full of business concern, scorn his apparent inactivity: 'The repose of the sun-embroidered green gloom slowly spread over my heart. I forgot for what I had travelled, and I surrendered my mind without struggle to the maze of shadows and songs. At last, when I [...] opened my eyes, I saw thee standing by me [...]/ How I had feared that the path was long and wearisome, and the struggle to reach thee was hard.'[43]

The pursuit of materialism stands in the way to the attainment of God, in this poem. It is, metaphorically, through the scorned and lonely path of being at one with nature that the speaker reaches his true destination. In other words, it is through the love of, and the delight one feels amidst, nature that the pilgrim succeeds in having a communion with God.

In poem 62 of *Gitanjali*, Rabindranath makes his view of the non-utilitarian as well as non-commercial aspect of nature quite clear[44]:

When I bring to you coloured toys, my child, I understand why there is such a play of colours on clouds, on water, and why flowers are painted in tints—when I give coloured toys to you, my child.

When I sing to make you dance I truly know why there is music in leaves, and why waves send their chorus of voices to the heart of the listening earth—when I sing to make thee dance.

When I bring sweet things to your greedy hands

> I know why there is honey in the cup of the flower
> and why fruits are secretly filled with sweet juice when
> I bring sweet things to your greedy hands.

The play of colours on clouds and on water, and music in the leaves and waves may not have any intrinsic commercial value, but to Rabindranath they are of great value in their own natural essence.

On the other side of nature stands the modern machine age with all the evils of industrialization, rapid commercialization, exploitation of natural resources and environmental degradation. These are the concerns of ecocritics in the contemporary world. In the name of the progress of civilization, when we find nature being ruthlessly exploited and the ecological balance disrupted, then a concerned citizen like Rachel Carson finds it imperative to step forward. She felt compelled, not only to critique the environmental crisis in *Silent Spring* (1962) but also to evoke the allegorical picture of a harmonious ecological relationship that existed earlier, between the human world and the natural world. She lamented the loss of the poetry associated with nature. It was the imagination of birdsong—celebrated in poetry for millennia—falling silent that initiated Carson's journey into the world of nature that was under siege from the human world. She was a scientist, yet Carson felt inspired to write against a scientific and technocratic culture that was bent on making an enemy of nature.

Birdsong has no value in this world. The extermination of different species, like the songbirds, in the name of this scientific culture, parallels in brutality the massacre of races of human beings in the days when European countries were creating an empire. Just as postcolonialism teaches us to condemn the so-called civilized and cultured white races for butchering native North and South American populations, and for enslaving, torturing and commercially exploiting masses of human beings belonging to the supposedly inferior races of Asia and Africa, ecocritics have taught us that it is inhuman of any part of the human society to erase traces of species and to take away the right of any nonhuman life form to live on earth. Today, ecocritics denounce anthropocentric dominance. More than a hundred years ago, Rabindranath, in the poems of *Gitanjali*, had shown respect to all existence. With the perception of a true sage-poet deriving inspiration from ancient Indian philosophy, he appreciated the essential unity in the existence of the living and the non-living as the true way of life.

It is to be noted that Rabindranath did not reject modernism and ask for a return to the pre-industrialized state of existence. He was realistic enough to acknowledge the necessity of the machine. The railway, the car and the machinery changing the face of England and putting that country on the forefront of human civilization were all duly noted by Rabindranath. In *Crisis in Civilization*, written at the end of his life, Rabindranath expressed a desire for the benefits of the machine, which helped England make such rapid progress, for Indians: '...mastery over the machine, by which the British have consolidated their sovereignty over their vast empire, has been kept as a sealed book, to which due access has been denied to this helpless country.'[45] At the same time, the excessive use of and dependence upon machines, or making the machine the master was what he dreaded. He felt anxious about the environmental and ecological costs of industrialization and unchecked urbanization.

Rabindranath visited England, other countries in Europe, and the USA, in 1912–13. It was during this period that the English translation of *Gitanjali* had been in circulation in the British literary and artistic world, leading to the award of the Nobel Prize in 1913. While Rabindranath was being feted in the Western society as a modern prophet of peace and calm, what, in his turn, did the poet from the East view that culture as? Rabindranath had delivered a number of lectures in the USA during this sojourn, and in these, we find a persistent critique of those ecologically disruptive values that he had equated with Western culture. He delivered a lecture titled 'The Relation of the Individual to the Universe' in America at this time, which soon became the first essay in *Sadhana* (1913). In this essay, he clearly pronounces his belief that the anti-nature stance was typically Western; it was ancient as well as modern. Its effect was felt all over the contemporary world and India had experienced it too[46]:

> The civilization of ancient Greece was nurtured within city walls. In fact, all modern civilizations have their cradles of brick and mortar.
>
> These walls leave their mark deep in the minds of men. They set up a principle of 'divide and rule' in our mental outlook... We divide nation and nation, knowledge and knowledge, man and nature. It breeds in us a strong suspicion of whatever is beyond the barriers we have built...

Rabindranath felt that the Western civilization meant division, disruption and unnecessary display of anthropocentric power. This anticipates much of the late twentieth and twenty-first century postcolonial and subaltern discourses and establishes the link between these two fields of study and ecocriticism. It is a critique of the dominant, metropolitan culture for its inclination towards alienating and destroying diverse races and nature as the 'other'. He wrote that in contrast to Western practice, the sustenance of the environment and ecology is characteristic of traditional Indian culture and civilization[47]:

> When the first Aryan invaders appeared in India, it was a vast land of forests... These forests afforded them shelter [...], pastures for cattle, fuel for sacrificial fire, and materials for building cottages...
>
> Thus in India it was in the forests that our civilization had its birth; and it took a distinct character from this origin and environment... Having been in

constant contact with the living growth of nature, his mind was free from the desire to extend his dominion by erecting boundary walls around his acquisitions... To realize this great harmony between man's spirit and the spirit of the world was the endeavour of the forest-dwelling sages of ancient India.

The question arises, however, that granted this ideal was noble and fitting for forest-dwelling sages and hermits, what happened when concern with material progress and prosperity became paramount for the rest of the people in that society, and cities were required for the growing complexities of life? Rabindranath seems to have anticipated this question: 'But even in the heyday of its material prosperity, the heart of India ever looked back with admiration upon the early ideal of strenuous self-realization, and the dignity of the simple life of the forest hermitage, and drew its best inspiration from the wisdom stored there.'[48]

Rabindranath's ecophilosophy prompted him to censure the Western propensity to construct a hierarchy, putting culture above nature[49]:

In the west, the prevalent feeling is that nature belongs exclusively to inanimate things and to beasts... According to it, everything that is low in the scale of beings is merely nature, and whatever has the stamp of perfection on it, intellectual or moral, is human-nature. It is like dividing the bud and the blossom into two separate categories, and putting their grace to the credit of two different and antithetical principles. But the Indian mind never has any hesitation in acknowledging its kinship with nature, its unbroken relationship with all.

Harmony is the essence of Rabindranath's ecological sensibility, in keeping with his estimate of the wisdom of the forest-sages. It is this lesson that the Upanishads had given him since his childhood. In contrast, the Western practice of constructing dissonance between human beings and nature was anathema to him. He repeatedly criticized the section of modern Indian society that aped these environmentally derogatory practices derived, primarily, from the British masters. To Rabindranath, it was not only a form of ignorance but also the harbinger of a self-destructive tendency. The serenity offered by his contemplation of ancient Indian ideals of ecological harmony was repeatedly disturbed by the harsh realities of the modern machine age. He wrote about this from his own experience.

What started as a personal response of shock and disgust at the sight of the pollution caused by factories near Calcutta, gradually turned into a sustained indictment of the machine. In 'The Modern Age', Rabindranath wrote[50]:

> Some years ago, when I set out from Calcutta [...] the first thing that shocked me, with a sense of personal injury, was the ruthless intrusion of the factories for making gunny-bags on both banks of the Ganges, The

blow it gave me was owing to the precious memory of the days of my boyhood, when the existence of a world which had its direct communication with our innermost spirit of beauty was the river. I was fortunate enough to be born before the smoke-belching iron-dragon had devoured the greater part of the life on its banks... when Calcutta, with her uplifted nose and stony stare, had not completely disowned her foster-mother, rural Bengal, and had not surrendered body and soul to her wealthy paramour, the spirit of the ledger, bound in dead leather.

Rabindranath felt disgruntled at the sight of Calcutta, his place of birth and the capital of India till 1911, because he perceived that it was being turned into a copy of the big factory-towns in England. The deadening effects of crass commercialization were replacing even the river he had loved since his childhood. It is as much from the standpoint of a practical criticism of imperialism as from the ecocritical point of view that his essay remains significant as a historical document[51]:

The reign of the machine and of method has been firmly established... This modern meeting of men has not yet received the blessing of God. For it has kept us apart, though railway lines are laid far and wide, and ships are plying from shore to shore to bring us together... The prevalence of the theory which realizes the power of the machine in the universe, and organizes men into machines, is like the eruption of Etna, tremendous in its force, in its outburst of fire and fume; but it is creeping lava... and its ashes smother life.

The first principle of ecology, as generally accepted, is that all elements in the world are interrelated. In Rabindranath's view, too, as in the ancient Indian philosophy, everything in the world is a manifestation of God. Hence, all were to be valued for their contribution to the formation of the whole. This whole represented divine unity. In this sense, modern ecological and ancient Indian philosophies intersect in his essay when he criticizes the modern machine-age for its dual harmful effect: first, it actually separates people and species, and creates artificial distance among human beings and between their world and the environment, even while reducing distances between geographical locations; second, it produces a spectacular display like an erupting volcano, but this is not life-sustaining. Thus, Rabindranath perceived, from both practical experience and philosophical wisdom, that the modern machine age, with its inclination towards the abuse of the environment and ecology, required sustained and dedicated critique for its excesses.

Rabindranath did not express the need he felt for harmonizing nature and culture in essays only. In 1922, he wrote the essay called 'The Modern Age' in *Creative Unity* to deplore the ugliness of the machine age. In May 1922, he also published *The Waterfall*, a play, in *The Modern Review*. The original Bengali play, *Muktadhara*, was written in January

1922. In this play, Rabindranath's ecological philosophy was given a vivid, dramatic representation. We will explore this play in depth, in the next chapter.

NOTES

1. Kripalani, *Tagore: Life*, 19–20.
2. Ibid., 21–22.
3. Dwivedi and Tiwari, 'Environmental Protection,' 163.
4. Ibid., 164.
5. Ibid., 164.
6. Misra, 'Man, Nature and the Poet,' 57.
7. Ibid., 57–58.
8. Ibid., 59.
9. Ibid., 59.
10. Bhattacharji, *Literature in the Vedic Age*, 229.
11. Misra, 'Man, Nature and the Poet' 59.
12. Ibid., 56–61.
13. Dwivedi and Tiwari, 'Environmental Protection,' 166.
14. Ibid., 167.
15. *Mahabharata* Mokshaparva 182.1–3 quoted in Dwivedi and Tiwari, 'Environmental Protection,' 168.
16. *Ibid.,* 169.
17. Bhagavad Gita 7.6 quoted in Dwivedi and Tiwari, 'Environmental Protection,' 169.
18. Tagore, *Journey to Persia*, 23. This is in the first chapter of the book translated by Surendranath Tagore for *Visva-Bharati Quarterly,* approved by Tagore.

19. Ibid., 24.
20. Misra, 'Man, Nature and the Poet,' 60–61.
21. Tagore, 'Shakuntala,' 237–251. It is necessary to make extensive references to this essay to explain Tagore's position vis-a-vis ecological practices in the ancient Indian context as reflected in literary texts.
22. Ibid., 240.
23. Ibid., 241.
24. Ibid., 241.
25. Ibid., 243.
26. Ibid., 243.
27. Ibid., 240–1.
28. Ibid., 240.
29. Ibid., 242–3.
30. Ibid., 244.
31. Ibid., 244.
32. Das, Introduction *Tagore: Selected Writings on Literature and Language,* 8–9.
33. Tagore, 'Shakuntala,' 246–7.
34. Ibid., 247.
35. Ibid., 249.
36. Das, Introduction *Tagore: Selected Writings on Literature and Language,* 2.
37. Egan, 'Shakespeare and Ecocriticism.'
38. This was a letter written to Indira Devi in Bengali and translated by her, reproduced in the Introduction to the *English Writings of Rabindranath* (henceforth consistently mentioned as *REW* and the relevant volume out of the four volumes) Volume 1 by Sisir Kumar Das. *REW* 1:11.
39. *Gitanjali* Poem 69 in *REW* 1: 66–67.
40. Das, Introduction *Rabindranath Tagore: Selected Writings on Literature*

and Language, 13–14.

41. Das, Introduction *Rabindranath Tagore: Selected Writings on Literature and Language,* 14.

In Sanskrit poetics, the theory of *rasa* has generated a significant critical concept. In the Upanishads, 'the ultimate Reality is the all-pervading existence (*sat*) the nature of which is absolute consciousness (*cit*) and delight (*ananda*). *Rasa* is the synonym of this absolute delight or *ananda*' (Sukla 93). It is possible to remember, in the context of artistic pleasure, Bharata's aesthetic concept of *rasa* enunciated in his treatise on dramaturgy called *Natyasastra*. An audience derives emotional sustenance or *rasa* from the experience of a performance or work of art that is not about emotion(s) of each individual, or of some individuals forming that audience. *Rasa* has a generalized significance. In the aforementioned interpretation of Upanishads too, *rasa* relates, not to one or some, but to the ultimate and all-pervasive existence. It is possible to interpret this all-pervasive existence, not always necessarily in religious terms, but as an equivalent to a spirit of universal love for the whole of the natural world. This celebrates human and nonhuman, living and non-living being on earth as manifestation of the all-pervading existence. However, unlike religion and philosophy that deal with such colossal generalization, in literature, it is customary to analyse and divide aspects of the world, human emotions and responses to local situations to smaller sections, easier to comprehend. Bharata highlighted situational factors causing eight primary emotions (*bhavas*) to give rise to corresponding *rasas* (*sringara* or the erotic, *hasya* or the comic, *karuna* or the sad, *raudra* or the violent, *vira* or the heroic, *bhayanaka* or the fearsome, *bibhatsa* or the revulsive and *adbhuta* or the marvellous) with *shanta* or the serene, or, at times, *vatsalya* or filial affection being described as the other *rasa*. Discussing Rabindranath's use of these ideas, Das wrote in Introduction *Selected*, 15–16:

> Scholars have written at length on the nature of rasa... Art is an instrument to attain *ananda*, joy, which is identical with *brahmasvada*, the 'savour' or perception of the supreme reality. Rabindranath uses the same terms to express his ideal of the ultimate 'savour' of art; but he does not accept the Vedantic position on the theory of rasa, nor does he negate the empirical world as illusion. As in philosophy so in art, he uses the metaphor of *sima* (boundary) and *asim* (boundless) to indicate how the two complement each other... The central theme of his philosophy, as Abu Sayeed Ayyub puts it, 'emerges as the notion that art is a bridge across the chasm which normally separates the individual from the world around'.

42. Tagore, *Gitanjali REW* 1:57.
43. *Ibid.,* 58.
44. *Ibid.,* 64.
45. Tagore, *Crisis in Civilization*, 15.
46. 'The Relation of the Individual to the Universe' *REW* 2:281.
47. ibid., 281.
48. Ibid., 281.
49. Ibid., 282.
50. 'The Modern Age' in *Creative Unity REW* 2:538.
51. Ibid., 542.

Chapter 3

Eco-ethics: *The Waterfall* (*Muktadhara*) and *Red Oleanders* (*Raktakarabi*)

In a note accompanying *The Waterfall*, Rabindranath wrote[1]:

> The waterfall around which the action of this play revolves is named Muktadhara—the Free Current. Such a descriptive name may sound strange in English, but those who are familiar with geographical names prevalent in India, will at once be reminded of the 'Pagla-jhora'—the waterfall of Darjeeling, whose meaning is the Mad Stream. The name 'Free Current' is sure to give rise in the readers' minds to the suspicion that it has a symbolical meaning; that it represents all that the word 'freedom' signifies in human life. This interpretation will appear to be still more obvious

when it is seen that the Machine referred to in the play has stopped the flow of its water.

In evoking the geographically real to present the symbolical, in a play about the confrontation between man and nature, Rabindranath creates a complex matrix of fact and fiction, real and ideal, and the natural and the artificial.

It is significant that *The Waterfall* elaborately describes the scene and setting. We read: 'In the background is represented the upper framework of a big iron machine; opposite to this is the sphere of the Bhairava temple, with its trident… After twenty-five years of strenuous effort [ ] royal engineer Bibhuti has succeeded in building up an embankment across the waterfall called Muktadhara.'[2] The juxtaposition of the sky-high machine and the trident of the temple seems to suggest that religious tradition and modern technology coexist peacefully. It appears to be more so when we read in the next few lines: 'The inhabitants of Uttarakut are seen visiting the temple with their offerings and preparing to hold in the temple courtyard the festival, which is to celebrate the achievement of the royal engineer, Bibhuti.'[3] But this apparent harmony is destroyed quickly when a stranger arrives and the dialogue presents a different view of the Machine[4]:

STRANGER. What's that there put up against the sky? It is frightful!… What's the object of the Machine?

A citizen informs him that it has bound up the waterfall

of Muktadhara. The Stranger's reaction is an indictment of the Machine from an aesthetic viewpoint[5]:

> STRANGER. What a monster! It looks like a dragon's skull with its fleshless jaws hanging down! The constant sight of it would make the life within you withered and dead!

The beauty in nature, symbolizing peace and harmony in ecology, is replaced by the Machine, which, the Stranger's words reveal, is an image of disruption and death. The Stranger criticizes the Machine for its audacious display, serving to disturb the aesthetic harmony of the landscape and challenge local cultural tradition and heritage: '…this isn't a thing to put up nakedly before the sun and stars. Can't you see how it seems to irritate the whole sky by its obtrusion?… Don't you think it's a sacrilege to allow it to overtop the spire of the Temple?'[6]

Soon, the aesthetic criticism of the Machine from an impartial visitor is replaced by the heartrending utterance of Amba, a poor woman who cries for her lost son Suman. Listening to her story, the Citizen informs her that he must have been working to build the embankment. A little later, it becomes clear that this has a sinister implication. The Messenger representing the Crown Prince Abhijit accosts Bibhuti, the royal engineer[7]:

> MESSENGER. You have been for a long time building up an embankment across the waterfall of Muktadhara.

Over and over again it gave way, and men perished smothered with sand and earth; and others got washed away by the flood...

BIBHUTI. When labourers became scarce in Uttarakut, I had all the young men of over eighteen years of age from every house of Pattana village brought out by the King's command, and a great number of them never returned to their homes. My Machine has triumphed against the storm of mothers' curses. He who fights God's own power, is not afraid of man's malediction.

The audience now realizes the horror of Amba's cries and understands why Suman could not return. The human cost of building this embankment becomes even more significant as it emerges from the level of the personal to encompass the universal, in the form of the tragedy that engulfed a whole generation of young men in a locality. Bibhuti's Machine, sponsored by Ranajit, King of Uttarakut, has snatched away the symbol of the future in the form of the lost youth and challenged the past in standing up against the religious tradition and sanctity of natural forces.

In the debate between Prince Abhijit's Messenger and Bibhuti, the political aspect of the nature of the Machine-building activity and the significance of the embankment as of great environmental consequence, become clear to the modern-day ecocritic[8]:

MESSENGER. The inhabitants of Shiu-tarai are still ignorant of this fact. They cannot believe that any man can deprive them of the water, which has been to them the gift of God.

BIBHUTI. God has given them the water; but He has given me the power to bind that water.

MESSENGER. They don't know that, within a week, their fields—

BIBHUTI. Why talk about their fields? What have I to do with their fields?

MESSENGER. Wasn't it your object to devastate their fields with drought?

BIBHUTI. My object was to make Man triumphant over the sands and water and stones, which conspired against him. I had not the time to trouble my mind about what would happen to some wretched maize fields of some wretched cultivator in some place or other.

MESSENGER. The Crown Prince asks you, if the time has not come at last for you to trouble your mind about it.

BIBHUTI. No! The pressure of water cannot break my embankment; the cry of hunger cannot sway my Machine.

Bibhuti's refusal to acknowledge hunger and drought as environmental consequences of the State decision, appears to be quite inhuman in the context of this play. Technology seems to work, personified in Bibhuti, as the handmaiden of coercive politics. We remember the Water Wars in our world when we read the play. Postcolonial ecocritics denounce such a combination of imperialism/neocolonialism and environmental exploitation. The robbery of the natural resources on which marginalized sections within a nation subsist, in the name of development activities proclaimed to benefit the whole nation's economy, is a political ploy evident in many parts of our world today. It often results in the complete loss of the means of livelihood and habitat for the marginalized people in a society, since they traditionally live closest to rivers and mountains and in forest-land. The rulers often perceive rivers in terms of dams, to control the flow of water in a particular territory in order to protect the interests of a privileged section close to those in power. Given the context of the play, the additional benefit of generating hydroelectric power by using the dammed up water, could not have been shown. Still, Rabindranath projected a situation that closely corresponds to the battle to control and exploit natural resources that is raging all over the world today.

In Rabindranath's play, the citizens of Uttarakut experience vicarious glorification due to their compatriot Bibhuti's achievement. They articulate the feeling, candidly, that to them, the Machine is a visible manifestation of their country's technological, cultural and racial superiority over the people of Shiu-tarai. These citizens raise Bibhuti up on their shoulders and sing[9]:

> We salute the Machine, the Machine!
> > Loud with its rumbling of wheels,
> > Quick with its thunder flame,
>
> Fastening its fangs
> > into the breast of the world

But there is an ethical cost to be borne for this victory over nature. The desire to dominate over nature and fellow human beings, it seems, turns the privileged or more powerful people into a selfish, monstrous entity that refuses to acknowledge the claims of environmental and human rights by the 'other'. In the play, the people of Uttarakut forget ethics in search of convenience and power. They used to love their Crown Prince Abhijit earlier, but they begin to thirst for his blood as soon as he opposes the dominant interest and takes up the cause of the people of Shiu-tarai. The Machine, which they claim is 'fastening its fangs into the breast of the earth', is cruel and anthropomorphic. The lack of a proper environmental imagination in the King, the Royal Engineer and their followers coexists with the erosion of human values in Rabindranath's play.

In *The Waterfall*, we learn that it is possible to disguise acts of coercion as political necessities. It is also noticeable that the people of Shiu-tarai are not included in the decision-making process and the political decisions are imposed from above. This appears to be a normal feature because there is a royal power and not a democracy in play, just as contemporary India was governed by the British Crown. Yet, by giving Bibhuti the type of rhetoric that is generally used by politicians, Rabindranath appears to discredit the entire process of imposing any kind of decision from above. What appears to be uncannily similar to this rhetoric of political expediency, used by Bibhuti, who is acting and speaking on behalf of the King, is the top-heavy decision-making process prevailing even in modern, democratic India. This has also been criticized by historian Ramchandra Guha, in 2000[10]:

> The environmental movement in India focuses too much on the products, and not enough on the *processes*, of development. Dams, even big dams, thermal power plants, and highways are not good or bad in themselves. They are neither the temples nor the hell-holes of India. The problem lies, rather, in the centralized and closed circle of decision-making. The broader masses of people in India have no role to play in deciding whether a dam should be built, how its catchments should be treated, how the populations displaced by it should be properly compensated, how its waters should be distributed and used.

The Waterfall is worthy of ecocritical acclaim for suggesting that there still exist humane and ethical ideals, and that following this path can guarantee prosperity for all, and thereby ensure peace in ecological relations. In *The Waterfall*, Crown Prince Abhijit opposes the royal decision to stop the flow of water to Shiu-tarai. He was most closely associated with the stream as he had 'come to know that he was not born to the royal house, but picked up near the source of this waterfall.[11] King Ranajit acknowledged that 'He began to visit the source of the waterfall alone, in the night. Once I surprised him, and asked him what was the matter, and why he was there. He said, "I find my mother's tongue in the murmurs of this water."'[12] He could feel the sorrow and bewilderment of the people of Shiu-tarai at the loss of what they had always considered to be the free gift of Mother Nature. Therefore, he could not accept the bondage of Muktadhara.

In order to keep Abhijit engaged, King Ranajit had sent him to Shiu-tarai as the governor soon after the Crown Prince had learnt of his relation with Muktadhara. Abhijit broke the barrier across the Nandi Pass, facilitating Shiu-tarai's attempt to reach places beyond Uttarakut, and to become independent. His decision to permit the people of Shiu-tarai to look beyond Uttarakut, which desired to keep it landlocked and in control, appeared suicidal—the mark of political immaturity. Therefore, the humanitarian outlook of Abhijit was not appreciated in Uttarakut. Rabindranath possibly highlighted this early humane act of Abhijit to show that he alone was meant to represent an eco-ethical worldview[13]:

> ABHIJIT. Every man has the mystery of his inner life somewhere written in the outer world. The secret of my own life has its symbol in that waterfall of Muktadhara. When I saw its movements shackled I received a shock at the very root of my being; I discovered that the

throne of Uttarakut is an embankment built up across my own life's current. And I have come out into the road to set free its course.

Crown Prince Abhijit refused to be bound by the earthly prospects of a crown and a kingdom and refused the companionship of Prince Sanjay, his brother and disciple. It seems that he felt that the course of action he had chosen for himself should be followed in seclusion and also that it was not for the general run of human beings. When Sanjay reminded him of a timid worshipper whose love came to Abhijit in the form of a single white lotus left at his seat, Abhijit acknowledged the bond of that love. Yet he declared that 'for the sake of that very love, which is in this world, I cannot tolerate this hideousness. It kills the music of the earth, and laughs its sinister laughter, displaying its rows of steel teeth in the sky. Because I love the paradise of the gods, I am ready to fight the Titans who menace it.'[14] To Abhijit, aesthetic sense and humane sensibility need to be complemented with eco-ethical action if one wanted to create a paradise on earth.

Abhijit's poetic farewell speech teaches his brother and disciple, Sanjay, the idea of environmental ethics, by referring to the contribution of the smaller life forms in the creation of our ecology[15]:

ABHIJIT. [...] Look at that tiny bird, sitting on the topmost branch of the pine tree, all alone. I do not know whether it will go to its nest, or take its journey

> across the night to a distant forest; but the sight of that lonely bird gazing at the last ray of the setting sun fills my heart with a sadness which is sweet. How beautiful is this world! Here is my salutation to all that has made my life sweet.

This description of the beauty of the sunset and the lonely bird is equivalent to a poetic coda. The first segment of the speech criticized the display of steel teeth. By juxtaposing the two pictures, Rabindranath made a powerful imaginative and literary statement about nature and human life. In Rabindranath's play, while the King and Bibhuti plan to rebuild the barrier across the Nandi Pass within a night to subjugate the rebellious crowd of Shiu-tarai in every possible economic and political way, Abhijit, acting alone, thwarts them. Sanjay informs the assembled friends and foes of the Machine, that Abhijit has broken the embankment[16]:

> SANJAY. Somehow he had come to know about a weakness in the structure, and at that point he gave his blow to the monster Machine. The monster returned that blow against him. Then Muktadhara, like a mother, took up his stricken body into her arms and carried him away.

While Cornucopian theorists would argue that the Machine was necessary, and Environmentalists would try to measure the economic benefits against the environmental cost involved, to find out how harmful, in the long run, such an embankment would prove to be, Deep Ecologists would propose an act of identification between nature and man, by means of an extension of sympathy. Long ago, Rabindranath had, through the different characters in *The Waterfall*, anticipated all these dissonant voices. And he had gone further. Through King Ranajit's comment at the moment he learned of the twin loss of the Machine and Abhijit, an enhanced understanding of the situation is given. It almost approximates Abhijit's act of environmental consciousness: 'I understand! And with this he found his freedom.'[17] With this reference, Rabindranath completes the circuit, linking the freedom of Abhijit to the freedom of the Waterfall.

∞

Rabindranath wrote *Red Oleanders* (1925) a few years after the publication of *The Waterfall*. It has a curious history. There were ten drafts of *Raktakarabi* in Bengali, which were prepared in 1923–24, but it was published in book form at the end of 1926, more than a year after the play released in English as *Red Oleanders*. The play is set in a Yaksha Puri, a miners' settlement. The miners are tantalized by the lure of gold and made to work until they perish. The King of the Yaksha Puri is extremely powerful and he prefers to stay behind an intricate iron lattice, letting the governors do the coercion on a daily basis to extract the maximum amount of work from the miners, whose identity and names have been erased. It is in this soul-killing environment that Nandini, a girl from a village, arrives. Nandini's natural exuberance creates a stir and changes the lives of all the citizens of the Yaksha Puri—from the King and his lackeys, down to the simple miners.

In *Red Oleanders*, the play begins with Kishor, an adolescent boy, bringing red oleanders to Nandini. When she implores him to return to work lest he should be late and face cruel punishment, he answers, 'You said you *must* have red oleanders. I am glad they're hard to find in this place. Only one tree I discovered after days of search, nearly hidden away behind a rubbish heap'.[18] Metaphorically speaking, in a world where search for tangible wealth is supremely important, it is not easy to find such love of natural beauty and simplicity. It seems that this is the reason why Kishor highlights the fact that the oleander tree could be found only by looking beyond the rubbish. Nandini sympathizes with Kishor and suggests that she herself should fetch the flowers and spare Kishor punishment by the masters for playing truant. But Kishor objects to this proposal[19]:

> KISHOR. Don't be cruel, Nandini. This tree is my one secret which none shall know [...] From now I shall have flowers which you'll have to take only from my hands.
>
> NANDINI. But it breaks my heart to know that those brutes punish you.
>
> KISHOR. It makes these flowers all the more preciously mine. They come from my pain.

Red oleanders—mere flowers—begin to symbolize both

nature and love from the very beginning. And integrally related to the process of such identification of nature with love is the young woman, Nandini, who inspires the whole action.

In the play, Kishor's adolescent adoration of Nandini is followed by the worship of the mature Professor of her beautiful existence. Nandini wonders aloud: 'What need have you of me?'[20]:

> PROFESSOR. If you talk of need, look over there!—
> You'll see our tunnel-diggers creeping out of the holes
> like worms, with loads of things of need. In this Yaksha
> Town all our treasure is of gold, the secret treasure
> of the dust. But the gold which is you, beautiful one,
> is not of the dust, but of the light which never owns
> any bond.

Nandini still cannot understand why they react to her presence in this way. In the Professor's explication—which comes as a reply to her query—the critique of the relative importance of the simple way of life and an artificial, sophisticated one, lies germane. The words paint a picture in which the sunlight gleaming through the forest thickets is considered to be hardly surprising but the light that breaks through a cracked wall is unexpected and therefore capable of awakening people to its beauty. Nature is an inevitable presence in a forest. However, in a totally artificial, materialistic culture, a flower—signifying the simple presence of nature—is so rare, that everybody in that society (from the young miner to the Professor, and later, even the King and his governors) responds when Nandini reminds them of its beauty, freshness, and the pristine purity of a natural environment untouched by man. In her turn, Nandini accuses the materialistic culture of the Yaksha Puri quite powerfully[21]:

NANDINI. It puzzles me to see a whole city thrusting its head underground, groping with both hands in the dark. You dig tunnels in the underworld and come out with dead wealth that the earth has kept buried for ages past.

PROFESSOR. The Jinn of that dead wealth we invoke. If we enslave him, the whole world lies at our feet.

Earth's bowels are rifled for what Nandini calls 'dead' riches. But as the play unfolds, we realize that this dead wealth does not bring satiety and happiness to anybody who covets it, either in itself or through the promise of power that it represents. The miners are expected to lose all semblance to humanity, they are treated like worms, and the sociopolitical system of the Yaksha Puri also dehumanizes them by reducing them to numbers, like prisoners. Living with heaps of gold, the simple villagers of yore, who have now turned miners, continue to pine for the living wealth of the golden harvest ripening in the fields outside the Yaksha Puri. The King is not seen, only heard—like a disembodied voice. And this adds to the mystery and terror of his power. Nandini, on behalf of the miners, tries to tell the King about the harvest song that infuses life into the moribund atmosphere there[22]:

> NANDINI. *Hark, 'tis Autumn calling:*
> *'Come, O, come away!'—*
> *Her basket is heaped with corn.*
> Don't you see the September sun is spreading the glow of the ripening corn in the air?
> *Drunken with the perfumed wine of wind, the sky seems to sway among the shivering corn, its sunlight trailing on the fields...*
> ...But can blocks of gold ever answer to the swinging rhythm of your arms in the same way as fields of corn? Are you not afraid, King, of handling the dead wealth of the earth?
>
> VOICE. What is there to fear?
>
> NANDINI. The living heart of the earth gives itself up in love and life and beauty, but when you rend its bosom and disturb the dead, you bring up with your booty the curse of its dark demon, blind and hard, cruel and envious. Don't you see everybody here is either angry, or suspicious, or afraid?

Nandini's whole being revolts against the rending of Earth's bosom for gold. It is as if other aspects of nature that form the vital source of our nourishment, physical, emotional and aesthetic, do not matter here. Red oleanders become important in this context. Nandini says that her lover Ranjan sometimes calls her 'Red Oleander'. Through the image of a mere flower, Rabindranath tries to suggest an eco-ethical way of life that opposes the materialistic culture that persists in viewing the natural environment as an entity that exists only to be exploited.

Rabindranath's play hinges on the incursion of Nandini, as an irresistible natural force, into the Yaksha Puri. In ecofeminism, wisdom lies in understanding the necessity of a symbiotic relationship between nature and the human society for the sustenance of life. It is expressed in terms of 'common human needs that can be satisfied only if the life-sustaining networks and processes are kept intact and alive.'[23] Nandini expresses utmost dismay when she finds that life-sustaining and life-enhancing forces of nature—the living golden harvest—are denied and shut out of the Yaksha Puri. Rabindranath uses the refrain of the song to remind us of this.

The centrality of Nandini, the quintessential woman who appears to be as irresistible as nature, is emphasized repeatedly in the play, especially since she acts as the agent of change in the perception towards both the natural and the cultural environment, among the inhabitants of the Yaksha Puri. Most notable is the change that the King undergoes. Inspired by her natural exuberance and celebration of the life force of the absent Ranjan, the King learns the language of love and natural harmony. He attempts to understand the futility of his greed for the dead gold and the power it brings over man and nature. Comparing himself with the as-yet-unseen Ranjan, the King, as the disembodied 'Voice', laments his own way of life[24]:

> VOICE. Shall I explain? Underground, there are blocks of stone, iron, gold—there you have the image of strength. On the surface grows the grass, the flower blossoms—there you have the play of magic. I can extract gold from the fearsome depths of secrecy, but to wrest that magic from the near at hand, I fail.

The tone of world-weariness suggested here is juxtaposed with his longing for love, life and the open joy of nature represented by Ranjan and Nandini. This, in turn, reminds us of some letters written by Rabindranath to C.F. Andrews from New York at the end of the year 1920. The sight of the splendour and opulence of the USA had generated a similar weariness as well as wariness in Rabindranath at the beginning of the decade in which he wrote both *The Waterfall* and *Red Oleanders*. The sentiment expressed throughout the latter almost echoes Rabindranath's letter, written on 13 December 1920, from New York, to Andrews in Santiniketan: 'Our Seventh Paus Festival at the Ashram is near at hand. I cannot tell you how my heart is thirsting to join you in your festival… My prayer is growing everyday more and more intense, to get away from the dark tower of unreality, from this dance of death trampling sweet flowers of life under its tread.'[25]

Even as we may recall that Rabindranath had to visit USA in search of money for the sustenance of his environment-friendly school in Santiniketan, we also learn that he disliked the excesses of a culture where pursuit of wealth seemed to have become more important than the consideration of the value of human life and happiness. A few years later, the King, as an important character in his play, also came to realize, like his creator, that it is possible for a great spiritual emptiness to exist in the midst of splendour. Rabindranath wrote on 17 December 1920 from New York[26]:

> Just now, I am on the top storey of the skyscraper to which the tallest of trees dare not send its whisper; but love silently comes to me saying: 'When are you coming down to meet me on the green grass under the rustling leaves, where you have the freedom of the sky and of sunlight and the tender touch of life's simplicity?' I try to say something about money, but it sounds so ludicrous and yet so tragic, that my words grow ashamed of themselves and they stop.

Money matters deaden life, and in *Red Oleanders*, through the King's lamentation over emptiness, Rabindranath's experience of the nature of modern life in a splendid city like New York seemed to have been given a symbolic representation.

In order to criticize the Yaksha Puri's acquisitiveness and consequent deadness of life, Rabindranath had written in the Preface to the Bengali version of the play, called *Raktakarabi*, about the significance of the figure of a single virtuous woman who comes to represent nature[27]:

> In the *Tretayuga*, Ravana, the powerful king with ambition and greed, used to capture many gods and goddesses, and make them work for his pleasure. But in the midst of his anti-god prosperity, suddenly appeared a woman [...] with the triumph of virtue... The Swarnalanka may, indeed, be traced in various places of the world, and at various levels. That the great poet (Valmiki) knew about that undefined and yet definite existence of Swarnalanka is beyond doubt (and) it was Kabiguru (the first poet Valmiki) who had stolen my story by means of his intuitive imagination, because... there are thousands of evidences that Swarnalanka is a thing precisely of our times.

As in the case of *The Waterfall*, where a reference to the geographically specific Pagla Jhora (Mad Stream) existing in Darjeeling, combines the real world with the literary and the symbolic dimensions within the play, so in this Preface, Rabindranath criticizes the excesses evident in contemporary materialistic culture. He deliberately juxtaposes the powerful king with the delicate woman in his play and, quite significantly, makes Nandini win the King over to the collective cause of survival and sustenance of the natural environment that she represents. Against the golden edifice of a whole culture, Rabindranath pits the puny mortal figure of a lonely woman: 'The entire play is an elaborate portrait of Nandini, a woman. She represents the joy of life, the simple beauty and pristine purity of Nature.'[28] In *Red Oleanders*, the King's voice articulates this vividly in terms of nature imagery, to compare—apparently quite paradoxically—his own vulnerability with Nandini's strength[29]:

> VOICE. One day, Nandini, in a far-off land, I saw a mountain as weary as myself. I could not guess that all its stones were aching inwardly. One night I heard a noise, as if some giant's evil dream had [...] suddenly snapped asunder. Next morning I found the mountain had disappeared in the chasm of a yawning earthquake. That made me understand how overgrown power crushes itself inwardly by its own weight. I see in you something quite opposite... The dance rhythm of the All... The rhythm... lightens the enormous weight of matter. To that rhythm the bands of stars and planets go about dancing from sky to sky, like so many minstrel boys. It is that rhythm, Nandini, that makes you so simple, so perfect. How small you are compared to me, yet I envy you... there are gifts that your little flower-like fingers can easily reach, but not all the strength of my body.

Nadini's power lies precisely in her being an embodiment of nature. The King and the governors of the Yaksha Puri had turned away from the beauty of nature to exploit it to accumulate wealth. In the process, they unwittingly imprisoned themselves in their barren, soul-killing golden cage. Ecofeminism tends to 'identify freedom with [...] loving interaction and productive work in cooperation with

Mother Earth.'[30] It celebrates women's 'most precious life force, which links them to each other, to other life forms and the elements. It is the energy that enables woman to love and to celebrate life... it is this magic which is contained within everything.'[31]

In the play, Nandini's almost magical life force is repeatedly mentioned. She is called a witch by Gokul when the tremendous potency of this force is felt but scarcely understood. Ecofeminists have repeatedly referred to the idea of a tremendous spiritual power: 'the female principle [...] permeating all things—this spirituality [...] as the life force in everything [...] akin to magic [...] [provides] insight into the existence of these all-embracing connections... through [which] ...powerless women could influence [...] powerful men...The ecological relevance of this emphasis on "spirituality" lies in the rediscovery of the sacredness of life.'[32] Rabindranath's ecophilosophy celebrates, through Nandini's love, the connectedness of all existence as an antidote to the excesses of a mechanical civilization.

In *Red Oleanders*, Rabindranath presented the problem of materialism and the exploitation of nature and less-privileged human beings through Chandra, a village woman-turned-miner. Her words resonate with the average person's longing for the lost principle of a simple and harmonious life in nature: 'In this season the villagers are preparing for their harvest festival. Let's go home.'[33] To her, while the vegetation and crops of her village constitute home, the mine, though a part of nature undoubtedly, does not merit mention as either natural or homelike. Her husband, Phagulal, and Bishu, another villager-turned-miner, remind her that the path leading back to the village has been closed by the King's deputy, the Governor. Evidently, the suave Governor, using religion and wine, creates a cultural environment that succeeds in keeping the miners enmeshed in his web of power. The gap between nature and culture appears to remain as it is, due to his machination. The path leading to the village was closed by the Governor because he needed to retain his workforce. But to a simple woman like Chandra, the nice behaviour and veneer of culture that he uses to achieve this end, make him look like generosity incarnate. Chandra pleads: 'Give us leave, Sir Governor, do give us leave. Let us go just for once, and see our waving fields of barley corn in the ear, and the ample shade of our banyan tree with its hanging roots. I cannot tell you how our hearts ache. Don't you see that your men here work all day in the dark, and in the evening steep themselves in the denser dark of drunkenness?'[34] In reply, the Governor, like any astute politician, speaks of his 'constant anxiety for their welfare' and fetches the High Preacher, Kenaram Gosain, whose honeyed words pacify Chandra.[35]

The words of a preacher are necessary to offer succour to the illiterate woman feeling disturbed at the severance from her natural roots. While Chandra tries to find peace and contentment in religion, the men try to stifle their urge to return to the village home, by drinking. As Bishu says: 'In this world there is hunger to force us to work;

but there's also the green of the woods, the gold of the sunshine, to make us drunk with their holiday-call… For me, nature's own ration of spirits is stopped; so my inner man craves the artificial wine of the marketplace.'[36] Evidently, the yawning gap between the natural and the artificial ways of life and culture cannot be bridged. However, Rabindranath still succeeded in raising questions, which, even though unanswered, remain crucial to our understanding of the relative importance of nature, culture and economy in any exploitative State. Chandra's simple question about their situation could translate into a basic question for our world too: Where is the materialistic civilization heading, at what cost is it heading there, and when, if ever, will it stop? When shall the exploitation of both the nature and the vulnerable section of the human species stop, and human beings and nature begin to coexist in harmony?

Chandra asks that since a huge pile of riches has been obtained, can things stop at last? Nandini's comrade, Bishu's answer to her question forms an indictment of an economy and culture based on greed and exploitation[37]:

BISHU. There's always an end to things of need, no doubt; so we stop when we've had enough to eat. But we don't need drunkenness, therefore there's no end to it. These nuggets are the drink—the solid drink—of our Gold King… Cups in hand, we forget we are chained to our limits. Gold blocks in hand, our master fancies he's freed from the gravitation of the commonplace, and is soaring in the rarest of upper heights.

The King tries to capture the essence of life and natural forces by engaging in his service both a physicist and an antiquarian, so as to encompass the past, present and future of human civilization. But he only learns about the limits of his own power from the study of history and science. The King realizes that he 'only burgles through one wall to reveal another behind it, and never reaches the inner chamber of the life spirit.'[38] It is this life spirit that prompted Ranjan to begin a digger's dance when he was subjected to tremendous pressure and torture to break his spirit, and which prompted Nandini, 'a girl wearing a grass-green robe', 'her mantle the green joy of the earth', to dismantle the grand edifice of the life-denying culture of the Yaksha Puri.[39]

In *Ecofeminism*, 'common human needs' are related with 'life-sustaining networks': 'In the usual development discourse these needs are divided into so-called "basic needs" (food, shelter, clothing et al) and so-called "higher needs" such as freedom and knowledge and so on. The ecofeminist perspective [...] recognizes no such division. Culture is very much part of their struggle for subsistence and life.'[40] At the end of *Red Oleanders*, it is in the name of a struggle for freedom, subsistence and a culture, which aligns itself with nature and life, that Nandini leads the workers and the King of Yaksha Town to fight against the Governor and his lackeys. It is true that as in the case of Crown Prince Abhijit in *The Waterfall*, as in *Red Oleanders* too, the protagonist has to sacrifice her life in the battle against the dominant power structure that plunders nature and persecutes marginalized human beings in the process. An indication of Rabindranath's thought is found in a lecture delivered by him in Argentina, in 1924. Leonard K. Elmhirst, his companion on that journey, had transcribed this lecture, in which, Rabindranath commented extensively on culture and the dominant human attitude towards nature: 'The background [...] is a world based upon the principle that each must fight the other, oppress or be oppressed, in order not merely that the ordinary simple needs of life may be satisfied, but that piles of accumulation may be set up.'[41] His speech anticipates the ecofeminist attempt to view all effort to survive in terms of both basic and so-called higher needs.

In his lecture, Rabindranath critiqued the King of the Yaksha Puri, who uses all his power to exploit indiscriminately and hoard the treasures of nature, human body and mind: 'the Great king exploits the resources of the underworld, of nature, of the mind, of science and of human physique and intelligence, using all the weapons of organization and the elaborate machinery of a highly centralized bureaucracy in order to add to his wealth. This wealth he measures in gold, or in souls, or in facts, or in human bodies.'[42] In other words, when Nandini comes into the Yaksha Puri, the practice had been to quantify everything and everybody. In a description of the King as sitting, hidden behind an elaborate lattice cover, and sucking the earth and the miners' life force dry, Rabindranath possibly suggests the sinister picture of a giant spider lurking, always vigilant, to suck the body juices of all the small creatures that fall into its web. In the lecture, Rabindranath used the idea of a busy hive: 'The King sits fascinated as he watches this hive, where everyone is busy, but no one content, where all are piling cell to cell, adding honey to honey, guarding the stores of accumulated wealth and efficient death-dealing stings, or casting out the human wastage, the drones, men who have been broken, or exploited.'[43]

English reviewers of *Red Oleanders* complained about the obscurity in its symbolical meaning. Rabindranath, in reply, sent a letter to *Manchester Guardian*, in which he linked Western imperialism and greed with the play's message, describing the twentieth-century political and economic exploitation or colonial situation. In this letter, he writes of the world as 'the world of Jack and Giant... not a gigantic man, but a multitude of men turned into a gigantic system... It is the organized pattern of greed that is stalking abroad in the name of (the) European civilization... its physiognomy blurred through its cover of an intricate network... against all direct human touch with barriers of race pride and [...] power'.[44] As a subject of the British colony, Rabindranath had been a close witness to the imperial politics of exploitation of a vast, marginalized population and the natural resources of India.

It is significant that Rabindranath's idea about the human and natural worlds, as presented through *Red Oleanders*, is not limited to an adverse criticism of the exploitative and imperialistic State policies only. It highlights a positive viewpoint through Nandini. In the lecture delivered in Argentina in 1924, Rabindranath's focus lay primarily on the positive aspects of the role played by Nandini, in harmonizing man with nature[45]:

> Into his hive flies the butterfly, armed with no sting, equipped with no power to gather or to store, but clothed in beauty, loving the light of day and life... Like strings on an untuned instrument they respond to her touch, and [...] here and there music and harmony come struggling forth, toils and troubles are forgotten, memories are aroused of the old scents and sounds, of the simple artistic colour and variety of nature, of the co-operative life of the village, where all were not numbers but neighbours, where there was music and beauty and life. But we have become numbers... Nandini then is this touch of life, the spirit of joy in life. Matched with Ranjan, the spirit of joy in work, together they embody the spirit of love.

To Rabindranath, Nandini is as essential as air and light. But he refers to our identifying numbers in the modern age. This suggests a palimpsest in which the modern acquisitive, industrial society continues to coexist with the symbolic world of *Red Oleanders*.

In the major part of the play, the King remains invisible. He also remains remote and, therefore, frightening. Yet, he realizes how barren his world is, even with the 'Midas touch'.

When Nandini asks, 'It is you who entangle yourself in your own net, then why keep on fretting?' the Voice answers: 'You will never understand. I, who am a desert, stretch out my hand to you, a tiny blade of grass, and cry: I am parched, I am bare, I am weary. The flaming thirst of this desert licks up one fertile land after another, only to enlarge itself—it can never annex the life of the frailest of grasses.'[46] It is in this realization of a basic self-contradiction inherent in his relationship with both nature and human beings that he finds the path leading to redemption. It is in order to relate to simple, non-utilitarian aspects of nature, which are evident in the spontaneity and magical touch of Nandini, that the King dismantles the visible marks of his power, breaking down the grand edifice behind which he used to lurk and crush overworked or rebellious miners. The King himself had become the unwitting tool, wielded by the Governor, who was earlier the King's instrument. The Governor duped the King into killing Ranjan unknowingly, though he had been awaiting a meeting with this young lover for long. It is the comprehension of what he had been made to do to Ranjan, whose identity had been kept hidden from him by the Governor and his supporters, that jolts the King into a realization of how he had had to sacrifice every humane consideration for a long time now, in order to consolidate his power and how, ironically, the system of coercion and terror had kept him imprisoned. The heart needs to undergo transformation first, Rabindranath seems to suggest, before anything else can change.

Rabindranath wrote a letter from New York on 25 December 1920, to C.F. Andrews in Santiniketan. The spirit of this later seems to relate perfectly with the theme of *Red Oleanders*[47]:

> Today is Christmas Day... But where is the spirit of Christmas in human hearts? The men and women are feeding themselves with extra dishes and laughing extra loud... These Western people have made their money but killed their poetry of life... Here, life is like a river that has heaped up gravel and sand and choked the perennial current of water that flows from an eternal source on the snowy height of an ancient hill... How to convince them of the utter vanity of their pursuits! They do not have the time to realize that they are not happy... My heart feels like a wild-duck from the Himalayan lake in the endless desert of Sahara, where sands glitter with a fatal brilliance but the soul withers for want of the life-giving spring of water.

It is possible to argue that this was essentially Rabindranath's idiosyncratic view of the West at a certain moment when he was feeling homesick for the open fields surrounding Santiniketan. But it could also be extended to understand an expression of his lifelong belief in frugality, simplicity and harmony in life. In *The Waterfall* and *Red Oleanders*, this ideal found a dramatic representation.

There is another way of reading *Muktadhara* and *Raktakarabi*: in the political context of India's ongoing struggle for Independence and Rabindranath and Gandhi's evolving ideas about science, technology and imperialism[48]:

> In the play *Muktadhara* (1922), Tagore presented an allegory about the prostitution of science for purposes of domination and exploitation. Exactly when he was engaged in the debate on the charkha, Tagore depicted in this play the revolt of the subject people to the construction of an enormous dam by alien rulers, a dam which would control the vital source of water, on which the life of the subject people depended...
>
> An analogous creation was the play *Raktakarabi* (1926), which reflects Tagore's deep concern about the exploitation of technology to extract profit from the labour of men, who are reduced to tools. The tyranny of the yantra-danava, the monster machine, was a recurring theme in Tagore's poetry as well.
>
> At the same time, when Tagore considered the role of science and technology, he spoke as an inheritor of the faith of (the) post-Renaissance era of Enlightenment... Tagore probably conceived of a via media between the two polarities, rejection of each gift of modern science and technology on the one hand, and passive unquestioning acceptance of it on the other...
>
> As for Mahatma Gandhi, a number of commentators have noted the evolution of his uncompromising position in *Hind Swaraj* towards a

> more complex and flexible stance typified by this statement in 1921: 'I am not aiming at destroying railways and hospitals, though I would certainly welcome their natural destruction... they are a necessary evil... Still less am I trying to destroy all machinery and mills.'

Pleading against the dissociation between the human and the natural, and between one section of the human society and another, did Rabindranath succeed in pointing towards an alternative? Abhijit's singular vocation of breaking down the embankment at Muktadhara could be one radical way of preserving the sanctity and distinctive identity of nature. His unconditional love for nature and the people downstream, in *The Waterfall*, could be appreciated by many environmental activists in their desire to see the rivers like Narmada unfettered. And Nandini's presence makes *Red Oleanders* a denunciation of those parts of the human society that, in moving away from living nature, exploit the earth to satisfy their greed by signing a Faustian pact not only with death individually, but also, with destruction and desolation of all humanity, cumulatively.

NOTES

1. *The Waterfall* REW 2:767.
2. Ibid.,165.
3. Ibid.,165.

4. Ibid.,165.
5. Ibid.,166.
6. Ibid.,166.
7. Ibid.,167.
8. Ibid.,167.
9. Ibid., 169.
10. Ramchandra Guha, Introduction. *The Use and Abuse of Nature*, xiii.
11. *The Waterfall REW* 2:170.
12. Ibid.,170.
13. Ibid.,178.
14. Ibid.,179.
15. Ibid., 179.
16. Ibid.,207.
17. Ibid., 207.
18. *Red Oleanders REW* 2:211.
19. Ibid., 211.
20. Ibid., 211–12.
21. Ibid., 212.
22. Ibid., 215.
23. Mies and Shiva, *Ecofeminism,* 13.
24. *Red Oleanders REW* 2:216.
25. Tagore, Letter of 13 December 1920 addressed to C. F. Andrews from New York, *REW* 3:270.
26. Tagore, Letter of 17 December 1920 addressed to C. F. Andrews from New York, *REW* 3:272.
27. Tagore, Preface to *Raktakarabi* tr. Ray, 237.
28. Ibid., 238.
29. Tagore, *Red Oleanders REW* 2:217.

30. Mies and Shiva, *Ecofeminism*, 13.
31. Ibid., 17.
32. Ibid., 17.
33. Tagore, *Red Oleanders REW* 2:222.
34. *Ibid.*, 222–3.
35. *Ibid.*, 223.
36. *Ibid.*, 219–20.
37. *Ibid.*, 221–222. We are reminded of Mahatma Gandhi's idea that the earth has enough for everyone's need, but not enough for everyone's greed.
38. *Ibid.*, 235.
39. *Ibid.*, 234–235.
40. Mies and Shiva, *Ecofeminism*, 13.
41. Leonard Elmhirst transcribed Rabindranath Tagore's lecture in Argentina as 'Red Oleanders: An Interpretation' in the *Visva-Bharati Quarterly*, New Series, 17 (November 1951) *REW* 4:336.
42. Ibid., 336.
43. Ibid., 336–7.
44. Rabindranath Tagore's letter to *Manchester Guardian* is 'Red Oleanders: Author's Interpretation' *REW* 4: 345–6.
45. 'Red Oleanders: An Interpretation' *REW* 4:337.

    In 'Festival of the Earth: Rabindranath Tagore's Environmental Vision,' an article by Nandan Dutta, available in the March 2007 issue of *California Literary Review*, we read: 'He sought a harmony between progress and preservation… Tagore's wariness of technology should not be taken as the whims of an irresponsible Luddite. He was deeply cognizant of the fact that technology when applied with discretion had the power to bring about great enhancement in the quality of human life.' Lack of knowledge of the machine could make a country like India remain backward, perpetuating underdevelopment and imperial domination, Tagore knew.

46. *Red Oleanders REW* 2:217.
47. This is found in 'Letters to a Friend' *REW* 3: 275.
48. Bhattacharya, Introduction *Mahatma and the Poet*, 32–33.

Chapter 4

In Search of Lost Harmony: Nature and Modernity in Rabindranath's Works

In the play involving Muktadhara, Rabindranath presented a warning against the fatal results of inequity and domination. He made it vivid through the collapse of the gigantic Machine constructed to mangle the earth's breast, challenge the sky and form an impediment to the free flow of water. In *Red Oleanders*, he contrasted the miners, who were compelled to dig the ground for the dead wealth called gold, which made a metallic click, with the farmers producing the living gold of ripe corn, whose beauty inspired the celebration of life with its music. In this, he indicated the distinction between two human tendencies. One suggests greed, exploitation, consumption and discord. The other signifies love, sharing, sacrifice and harmony. Together, the first group of human propensities seem to describe the steps necessary for the modern civilization to reach the pinnacle of material success. The other, however, does not always lead to success in the worldly sense, but it keeps human beings humane. Rabindranath hailed the modern age for its scientific and technological knowledge but lamented it too, thinking of the discord that it has created. And yet, without understanding the modern conditions giving rise to this discord, harmony cannot be reestablished in nature and human life.

In 1933, Rabindranath delivered three lectures at the Andhra University. Together, they are called 'Man'. In these lectures, Rabindranath recorded[1]:

> Discords become too evident when the tuning of the instrument is going on, but they are not a part of the music itself. Discords jar on us, and if they did not, we should not progress on our quest after harmony. That is why we give the name 'Rudra', or Terrible, to the Infinite—He draws us towards freedom along the path of the pain of disharmony.

In his childhood, it was a cohesive world of harmony and music that Rabindranath experienced in terms of his love of nature and the ancient philosophical precepts. This experience found its culmination in the poems of *Gitanjali*, composed when he had reached nearly fifty years of age. He began to understand that disharmony existed in the relationship between man and nature, and within the human world, when he was nearly thirty years old. This sorrow was a constant factor in his life. At the same time, an implicit trust in the one God amidst all personal and collective trials remained the mainstay of his life. Hence, the juxtaposition of the modern manifestation of discord and the traditional love of nature and harmony shaped his responses to life.

Rabindranath did not formulate an ecocritical theory. Rather, he lived and wrote, throughout his life, a story of ecological sustenance. In order to trace the contours of his ecological thought, five interconnected ideas might be found in his work. They are unity (suggesting relationship), simplicity (suggesting humility), surplus (suggesting creation), service (suggesting love) and freedom (suggesting spontaneous cooperation). Rabindranath repeated these ideas in his essays and lectures for decades and these values were enshrined in his fiction, drama and poetry, as also in his 'life's work' at Santiniketan and Sriniketan, around the concept of Visva-Bharati.

In 'The Second Birth', a lecture delivered in America during Rabindranath's visit there in 1916–17, and later published as part of a book called *Personality* in 1917, Rabindranath discussed, at length, the basic unity and interconnectedness of all life and nonliving things in the universe, as a philosopher. And yet, like a practical man, he also wrote about how man thinks of himself as the centre of the universe and views everything outside his own limited self as 'alien' or the Other: 'For us, inanimate nature is the outside view of existence. We only know how it appears to us, but we do not know what it is. For that we can only know by sympathy'.[2] But this question of the division and distinction between the human self and nature as the Other should not arise at all, according to him, if man understands the real meaning of life: 'the curtain rises, life appears on the stage, and the drama begins... We know what life is, not by outward features, not by analysis of its parts, but by a more immediate perception through sympathy. And this is real knowledge.'[3]

Rabindranath expressed an expectation that our perception of life should be direct and immediate and not for the sake of remote scientific or philosophical disquisition. He then analysed the history of the evolution of life forms on earth in order to show how a concept of unity emerges even out of the apparent dualism of the idea of the human self and nature as the other[4]:

> We see a tree... Its life is based upon a dualism—on one side, this individuality of the tree, and on the other, the universe. But if it were a dualism of hostility and mutual exclusion, then the tree would have no chance to maintain its existence... It is a dualism of relationship. The more perfect the harmony with its world of the sun and the soil and the seasons, the more perfect the tree becomes in its individuality. It is an evil for it when this interrelation is checked. Therefore life, on its negative side, has to maintain separateness from all else, while, on its positive side, it maintains unity with the universe. In this unity is its fulfilment.

If the tree is considered to be a simple life form that cannot move or express its feelings, then the next and higher stage is, of course, animal life. Rabindranath shows that here too, the same principle of unity holds supreme[5]:

> In the life of an animal on its negative side this element of separateness is still more pronounced, and on that account on its positive side its relationship with the world is still wider. Its food is more fully separated from it than that of the tree. It has to seek it and know it under the stimuli of pleasure and pain. Therefore it has a fuller relationship with its world of knowledge and feeling... In the trees the separation from their progeny ends in complete detachment, whereas in animals it leads to a further relationship. Thus the vital interest of animals is still more enlarged in its scope and intensity, and their consciousness is spread over a larger area. This wider kingdom of their individuality they have constantly to maintain through complex relationship with their world. All obstacles to this are evils.

If, from the simple question of the need for unity of the self and the universe for the sake of existence (as in the case of a tree), Rabindranath moves on to the more complex interplay of knowledge and feelings in the case of animals, which is necessary for their survival, can the even more conceptually complex question of human existence on earth lie far behind?

Rabindranath says, 'In man, this dualism of physical

life is still more varied. His needs are not only greater in number and therefore requiring larger field of search, but also more complex, requiring deeper knowledge of things. This gives him a greater consciousness of himself.[6] The moment this question of the great human consciousness arises, apparently the wider grows the gulf separating man from other things, like the tree and the animal. Taught as we are to view man as the greatest and best possible life form, courtesy the Western, Biblical tradition of thinking of the world in terms of anthropocentrism, it becomes difficult to accept any idea but the one prompting man to control and consume trees and animals. Man has also destroyed them at will, sometimes in the name of necessity, citing industrialization and urbanization, but often irresponsibly, in a display of power. Apparently, it is a story of dualism manifested in terms of man not as part of nature, as in the case of the trees and animals. They are governed by natural rules that foster their interrelated existence as this is necessary for the individual's survival. But from the human perspective, apparently, it is most often a story of man versus the trees, the animals and the inanimate things, collectively called nature.

Rabindranath was keenly aware of the apparent dichotomy between a sense of human superiority over other living beings, and a sensibility of the necessity to coexist with the nonhuman features of earth, for the sake of survival. If it is the existence of the human mind and soul that separates him from the world of vegetation and animals, because the latter have bodies and appetites only, then, Rabindranath suggested, it is the existence of the same higher mental and moral faculty in human beings that forges a link between the human self and nature as the other[7]:

> It is his mind which more fully takes the place of the automatic movements and instinctive activities of trees and animals. This mind also has its negative and positive aspects of separateness and unity. For, on the one hand, it separates the objects of knowledge from their knower, and then again unites them in a relationship of Knowledge. To the vital relationship of this world of food and sex is added the secondary relation which is mental. Thus we make this world doubly our own by living in it and by knowing it.
>
> But there is another division in man, which is not explained by the character of his physical life. It is the dualism in his consciousness of what is and what ought to be... What is desired dwells in the heart of the natural life, which we share with animals; but what should be belongs to a life which is far beyond it [...] So, in man, a second birth has taken place.

If man is defined not merely in terms of appetites but in terms of morality, as Rabindranath does here, then by definition, humanity is inclusive of just and ethical behaviour towards each and everything in the world. However, the question is not so simple. Rabindranath wrote about the conflict between an individual, human desire for controlling what is and the equally distinctive human desire to establish what should be. Rabindranath wrote that the problem lies in the magnitude of the conflict. Paradoxically, it makes human existence in, and humans' relationship with, the world, meaningful[8]:

> Many things that are good for the one life are evil for the other. This necessity of a fight with himself has introduced an element into man's personality, which is character. From the life of desire, it guides man to the life of purpose. This life is the life of the moral world [...] In this moral world, we come from the world of nature into the world of humanity.

For man, it is not enough to be an anonymous part of nature; it is not even satisfying to control nature all the time. Morality prompts man to establish a unique relationship with nature, based on mutual respect and ethics. I believe that it is in the world of such humanity that Rabindranath's play *Muktadhara* becomes meaningful. Pitted against a selfish desire for political domination, which sought to reduce both human and natural resources to instruments of power, Prince Abhijit comes to represent Rabindranath's philosophy of nature and life in terms of morality and humanity as indices of true human identity, reflected in his sacrifice, in his attempt to reintegrate human and natural existence.

Rabindranath felt that where an animal has responsibility only towards its own existence, man's struggle for existence involves him deeper in nature[9].

> For all other creatures, nature is final. To live, to propagate their race and to die is their end. And they are content... In man, the life of the animal has taken a further bend. He has come to the beginning of a world, which has to be created by his own will and power... Even his physical needs are not supplied to him ready-made in nature's nursery. From his primitive days, he has been busy creating a world of his own resources from the raw materials that lie around him... Thus we find that man is not content with the world that is given to him; he is bent upon making it his own world. And he is taking to pieces the mechanism of the universe to study it and to refit it according to his own requirements.

This kind of a presentation of human aspirations and activities remind us of the Cornucopian theory, which tells us that as man wants to make his world more and more habitable, he faces challenges and, in the power of science and technology, the solutions and means for progress are to be found. This basic human motivation assumes the form of a search for a world that he wants to make perfectly hospitable. It prompts him to explore, exploit and shape nature as a resource. Nature becomes something necessary in the act of moulding the world for the fulfilment of human requirements. As from the angle of the Cornucopian theory, so also from the perspective of common sense, it appears that this attitude is necessary for both the survival and the prosperity of the human society in an inhospitable world. Rabindranath never denied its necessity. However, he moves beyond the concept of man as scientist/technocrat to highlight that aspect of man which separates him from an animal in terms of morality. This concept is not just based on the idea of animals having an amoral appetite and human beings behaving in an immoral manner to gain power and material possessions by exploiting a section of the human society and nature as resources. Rather, it is based on the idea of morality itself. In 'The Second Birth', Rabindranath wrote[10]:

> In the natural world, with the help of science, man is turning the forces of matter from tyranny into obedience.
>
> But in his moral world he has a harder task to accomplish. He has to turn his own passions and desires from tyranny into obedience. And continual efforts have been directed towards this end in all times and climates. Nearly all our institutions are outcome of these endeavours.

Rabindranath would have acknowledged and yet moved beyond the plea of expediency presented by the supporters of the Cornucopian theory as well as the Capitalists. His ideas also appear to anticipate certain aspects of Deep Ecology. In *Raktakarabi*, for instance, the Yaksha Puri possibly represents man's success in 'turning the forces of matter from tyranny into obedience.' Simultaneously, however, in Nandini's company, we also find the King attempting the harder task of turning 'his own passions and desires from tyranny into obedience.' At the end of the play, the web of desire and deceit, created by a few privileged human beings trying to exploit nature and rural people, is attacked by a section of the human society itself. The lingering impression at the closure of the play is of the autumn song—the song of human love and longing for the open sky and the ripening corn—that symbolizes the unity of the human and natural worlds.

Loving nature and working according to a code of ethics based on love for all that is in existence, is the basis of the feeling of unity that Rabindranath upheld. Moral uprightness coupled with this love, helps to free a human being from the bondage of physical rules of pleasure and pain and strengthens the mind in such a way that man transcends thoughts of mere physicality and immediate gain. In other words, man gains freedom from selfish thoughts and emotions: 'I become more in my union with others... [W]hen different personalities combine in love [...] then it is not like adding to the horse power of efficiency, but [...] what was imperfect finding its perfection in truth, and [...] joy; what was meaningless, when unrelated, finding its full meaning in relationship.'[11]

In his literary work, Rabindranath always upheld the basic idea of unity among the different manifestations of life in the world, and of making possible a harmonious coexistence of all, through love. This had taken various forms since the earliest period of his writing career. Sometimes, there would be a half-articulation of the recognition of the bond between nature and man by some of his fictional characters, as in *Rajarshi*, an early work, and sometimes the recognition of this fact would be articulated more clearly. In 'Brikshabandana' ('Hymn to the Tree'), the poem composed in Santiniketan on 23 March 1927, and collected in *Banabani* in 1931, Rabindranath writes[12]:

> O brave earth-child,
> You declared battle to free earth's soil
> From the desert's dread fortress....
> On rock-tablets you wrote the tale of triumph
> With leaf-letters: you charmed the dust,
> Drawing your own path on traceless fields....
> You wrought in your branches the primeval
> Shelter of song...
> ...Therefore to your shelter
> I come to gain the sacrament of peace...
> ...To receive the open,
> Generous forms of life, rasa ever new-formed...

The poet is one who, like the forest hermits in the Vedic age, wants to decipher the language of the living beings on earth. This desire to communicate and cherish the unity of the individual with the world is expressed in short stories too.

In one short story, in particular, it is the silent love for nature that forms a deeply moving picture. 'Subha' (1893) has a mute (but not deaf) girl as the protagonist.

Rabindranath portrayed an extraordinarily sensitive picture of this rural girl, who, in the human world, was considered to be something of an anomaly. In the nineteenth-century society in Bengal, all young girls were evaluated carefully by the family members of the prospective bridegroom, before and after marriage, for any physical lapse or shortcoming in behaviour. And social norms had made it mandatory that the girls be married off at an early age. Possibly, the idea of blame from all 'normal' people in the society for giving birth to a mute girl, who would be difficult to marry off, and the fear for her dark future prompted Subha's family to criticize her 'as a curse sent by God... Her mother, in particular, thought of her daughter as a lapse on her own part [...] was always displeased with her.'[13] In an atmosphere where even the mother felt it difficult to show affection to a mute girl, Subha would find respite from her suffering, in the world of nature: 'Nature seemed to [...] speak for her. The gurgling of the stream, the clamour of people's voices, the boatmen's songs, the calls of the birds, the rustling of the trees: all these [...] the movement, the stir, would come and break like waves of the sea on the ever silent shore of the girl's heart.'[14] It may be noted that, to Subha, the sounds and movement that constitute nature include the human sphere of activities too. In other words, a perfect ecology, or coexistence of the human and nonhuman elements in nature, generates her perception of life and establishes itself as the object of her love.

Subha is not able to communicate her love for her

parents in words, but she does not find it difficult to love the environment and nonhuman life in her village, wordlessly. Rabindranath's language indicates that not only was Subha permitted to love nature but also that her 'intimate friends' from nature reciprocated her love freely[15]:

> There were two cows in the cattle-shed... They had never heard their names uttered by the girl, but they knew her footsteps... They could understand, better than her fellow human beings, when Subha was being loving... When she was made to hear hard words in the house, she would come to these two dumb friends of hers—and from her long-suffering, melancholy-stilled gaze, they would seem to fathom the girl's heartache [...] standing close to her and rubbing their horns against her arms to comfort her with wordless solicitude.

In the human world, Subha's tears and eloquent eyes have no value. Her silence, interpreted as a sign of modesty by the members of the bridegroom's family, helped them choose her for marriage. But when the truth was revealed after marriage, she was spurned by everybody, including her husband, as a cheat, though she had done nothing to entice or dupe them into this marriage. Actually, she did not want to marry at all and was desperately unhappy at the thought of being uprooted from the only place on earth where she had known love, at least from nature. It is to be noted that Rabindranath presents Subha as anthropomorphizing nature habitually. It is possible, on the one hand, to dismiss this as an ignorant villager's superstition, but, on the other, it could also be interpreted as the finest sensibility of love represented in literature. On the eve of her departure to the rented house in Calcutta for her wedding, Subha 'fell on the grass as if to clasp the earth, this huge unspeaking mother of mankind, with both her arms and to say, "Mother, don't let me go. Spread out your two arms like mine and hold me to you."'[16]

Subha's bond of love with the soil, water, plants and animals in her native place is strong. But she was not permitted to live in peace and harmony in this environment, as she suffered from the double disadvantage of being mute and a girl of marriageable age. Her feelings would not be considered practical or of any value to anybody, ever. Her inclination to spend most of the time amidst nature and in the proximity of cows would rather be interpreted as the desire to identify herself with nature that is, practically speaking, as 'dumb' as her own self. Yet, Subha, in spite of her silence, proves herself to be a fine human being, sensitively attuned, precisely through her silent love of nature. This uprooting from the bosom of nature hastens her death after marriage.

If we feel that Subha's story of love of nature, though pathetic, is of no practical use, then we need to remember another story written by Rabindranath soon after. This story was also set in rural Bengal. In 'Trespass,' Jayakali Devi, a widow, has such a commanding presence that 'with a few words, or sometimes even without words, she could often silence the most talkative of men... While her husband was alive, the property attached to the temple had almost been lost. The widow managed to recover all pending payments, sort out boundary disputes, and evict old encroachers to bring things back in order.'[17] Rabindranath presents her in the story as: 'This stern woman [who] stood poised above the village like a tall staff of divine justice, ready to strike.'[18] Since she was a childless widow, Jayakali lavished her attention and care on the idol at the temple: 'Under Jayakali's care, the temple yard looked spotlessly clean, without a stray blade of grass anywhere.'[19] In other words, she was adept in keeping all components of both the human and natural domains in the village, in her control.

Jayakali is presented as the sort of person who does not tolerate even a dry leaf to linger on the Madhabi creeper. She does not permit the children to enter or the goat to feed inside the temple yard. '[T]he hungry young goat had to return from the gate bawling for its mother, having tasted nothing but the stick.'[20] When this strict woman, who was not known to show affection to anybody or anything, would enter the temple, she would transform herself completely in total surrender to the idol. 'In front of the idol she was soft, deferential... utterly submissive... It was her husband and her son, her entire world.'[21] As readers, we now understand why she defended the temple premises from everybody so strictly. She was unsparing to her nephew, a child, who faced severe punishment when he trespassed on that yard.

She locked the boy up and starved him. The idea was not to let anybody or anything pollute the place where her idol resided. Yet when a dirty pig, anathema to a pious Hindu widow like her, hides behind the Madhabi trellis from a 'drunken mob of untouchables' in order to survive, she bolts the temple gate from inside, to save the animal.[22] The crowd pursuing the pig, 'could not believe, even though they had seen it with their own eyes, that Jayakali would shelter an unclean creature in the temple of her Radhanath.'[23] What could have caused this deed but a sudden surge of pity and empathy for the cowering pig, even though it was the most unclean of life forms to her? In this context, Coleridge's 'The Rime of the Ancient Mariner' might be recalled. The Mariner had killed the albatross gratuitously and was leading an accursed existence. Much later, only when he blessed the slimy water snakes spontaneously, did the curse lift. In the poem, this spontaneous blessing is described in terms of a sudden outpouring of love for all living creatures. In Jayakali's case, did Rabindranath want to suggest a sudden and similar surge of love for the animal in her mind that washed away considerations of religion, status and custom? Rabindranath does not relate her action to her position as a childless woman. In other words, it does not seem as if he is suggesting that a sudden upsurge in her dormant maternal instinct made her ignore social taboos to protect an animal that was shaking like a helpless child. Rather, it seems from Rabindranath's words at the end of the story, that her decision to save the pig had something to do with her sense of its being one of God's creatures too. The narrator of the story is revealed to be omniscient, and in this capacity, the comment at the end of the story comes as: 'This small incident brought great satisfaction to the great God who looks after all creatures of the universe; but the petty village god, called the community, felt considerably perturbed.'[24]

If we consider Subha's disability and her silent as well as sustained communion with nature, and the sudden upsurge of empathy for a life form in Jayakali, it appears that Rabindranath is presenting them as counterpoint to a narrow sense of culture. To him, the highest mark of civilization is perhaps to live in harmony with everything and everybody in one's environment and ecology. These stories tell us of the lives of two obscure women in rural Bengal at the end of the nineteenth century. There cannot be any far-reaching environmental activism in their life. But it is environmental activism that would be necessary to reverse the trend of destroying one's ecological community. From 1901, though, Rabindranath himself would generate, in Santiniketan-Sriniketan, such environmental ethics in action. In a way, by representing the voice of nature, usually unheard, in these two short stories, he awakens us to a different dimension of human perception of nature, in terms of harmony, love and cooperation.

Rabindranath wrote extensively on how love makes us perfect and whole, reintegrating human beings with an existence that is larger and deeper than our limited, selfish selves. He combined the concepts of unity, love and perfection to signify the path towards God[25]:

> The feeling of perfection in love, which is the feeling of the perfect oneness, opens for us the gate of the world of the Infinite One, who is revealed in the unity of all personalities; who gives truth to sacrifice of self, to death which leads to a larger life, and to loss which leads to a greater gain... In this we become conscious of the relationship between what is in us and what is beyond us.

Rabindranath is clearly and frankly pantheistic here, viewing both nature and human life or rather, all existence as a manifestation of God and, hence, considering them spiritually or in essence as united, full of love and harmony and as potentially perfect. He quoted the Sanskrit scriptures to illustrate this idea: 'Know all that moves in the moving world as enveloped by God.'[26]

If human beings are to be considered in the light of the all-pervasive presence of God, then we are surrounded by the same life that envelopes the nonhuman existence. Recognition of this fact is the first necessity. Rabindranath wrote about the responsibility of human beings towards such existence[27]:

> It is not for him to be merely the recipient of favours from nature; he must fully radiate himself out in his creation of power and perfection of love. His movement must be towards the Supreme Person,

> whose movement is towards him. The creation of the natural world is God's own creation, we can only receive it and by receiving it, make it our own. But in the creation of the spiritual world we are God's partners... With him our relationship as mere receivers of gifts is not fully true, for that is one-sided and therefore imperfect relationship. He gives us from his own fullness and we also give him from our abundance.

Reciprocity in love and service, rendered and received mutually, thus becomes not only synonymous, but also the spiritual essence of our communion, with both nature and God, and creates the concept of real freedom as the freedom to cooperate with all that exists, without inhibition of any kind, to make life meaningful.

In *Gitanjali* (poem 14), Rabindranath suggested that human beings stand in awe of God, because the contemplation of the all-pervasive power of God reveals the truth that man is saved from all those activities that make us less free, less loving and less human, by Him: 'My desires are many and my cry is painful, but ever didst thou save me by hard refusals [...] Day by day thou art making me worthy of the simple, great gifts that thou gavest to me unasked—this sky and the light, this body and the life and the mind—saving me from the perils of overmuch desire.[28]

Rabindranath's ideas of looking beyond chances of the immediate gratification of selfish human desire and looking at the world with love are important for our understanding of the essential unity of man and nature. In addition, his language suggests that man's selfish desire to dominate nature and his lack of humility makes him less human. It is possible that a similar reason had prompted him to pray to God in *Gitanjali* (poem 36) in this way: 'This is my prayer to thee, my Lord—strike, strike at the root of penury in my heart... Give me the strength to make my love fruitful in service.'[29] In other words, Rabindranath asked for humility in attitude towards all that exists, and the excision of pride from his heart. Pride blinds us to the true relation between ourselves and others. The result is a barren world like that experienced by the King in *Raktakarabi*. Only love and empathy can save us from such isolated, and, hence penurious, emotional existence. If, emerging from the web of selfish desire and pride, we humbly think, with love, of serving God and all in His creations, including all human and nonhuman beings, as our moral duty, then the true joy of life might be experienced, Rabindranath seems to suggest the same in *Gitanjali* (poem 73)[30]:

> Deliverance is not for me in renunciation. I feel the embrace of freedom in a thousand bonds of delight.
>
> Thou ever pourest for me the fresh draught of thy wine of various colours and fragrance, filling this earthen vessel to the brim.
>
> My world will light its hundred different lamps with thy flame and place them before the altar of thy temple.

> No, I will never shut the doors of my senses. The delights of sight and hearing and touch will thy delight.
>
> Yes, all my illusions will burn into illumination of joy, and all my desires ripen into fruits of love.

Rabindranath's ideas regarding man, morality and nature appear to belong to the realm of poetry and philosophy. In other words, it is possible to interpret his ecological ideals in terms of what should be. The question arises as to whether these ideals have any relevance at all in the complex, industrialized, modern world—the world as it is?

In 1934, Gilbert Murray, in a letter to Rabindranath, had raised the question of how far the latter had accepted 'the machine'. The correspondence between Murray and Rabindranath in this context was published as 'East and West'. Here, Murray proposed that intellectuals of the East and the West could well differ in their opinion regarding the use of machines and nature, and yet this should not prevent them from cooperating for the sake of improving international relations. Murray was actually quite specific about what he considered to be Rabindranath's anti-machine worldview[31]:

> I have just been reading your play called in French 'La Machine', and I see in it, if I am not mistaken, your hatred of machines as such, and of all the mechanization of modern life. Now I happen to admire machines and the engineers who make them. I respect their educational influence. I feel that if a boy's horse

or dog will not do what he wants he will probably try to make it do so by losing his temper and beating it; but if his bicycle or his wireless will not work, he knows it is no good losing his temper. He has to think and work, to find out what is wrong and to put it right: which is a priceless lesson for any boy. Then the use of machinery teaches conscientiousness to the mechanic. I often think of the thousands and thousands of aeroplanes that are plying their daily tasks throughout Europe and America; each one of which must be properly adjusted and made fast by the workmen before the machine starts. A mistake, almost any mistake, is quite likely to be fatal. But the engineers, quite ordinary men for the most part, are so trained that they do not make a mistake... I write this not to argue but merely to illustrate; to show that difference of opinion, habit or training need not cause alienation. You can remain profoundly Indian and I a regular Westerner, without disturbance to our mutual sympathy.

Murray seems to feel that Rabindranath was entitled to nurture a hatred of machines as an Indian, while a Westerner could continue to dominate over air and earth with his machinery. Yet, in a way, Murray seems to have apologized for the greed for power in the run-up to the First World War and the ravages perpetrated on the earth by means of the same machine when he wrote also of his 'poor distressed civilization' that had made the 'most ghastly war in history', yet 'hated itself for doing so', still feeling afraid of its 'baseness and savagery.'[32] Murray was an optimist because he still had 'hope for the future of this tortured and criminal generation' but at the same time, he felt that at the sight of the excesses of the West, Rabindranath, in the East, would be justified to 'have lost hope' and to 'prove right' about it.[33]

Rabindranath's reply is an indication of his profound understanding of the question, not only of a mechanized, modern world and a supposedly primitive, peaceful East, but of a world situation where machine and modernity were necessary everywhere. Yet, he also explicated his reservations regarding the Machine Age and warned against its abuses, linking the whole question to the exercise of morality in man's relationship with his environment[34]:

> My occasional misgivings about the modern pursuit of Science is directed not against Science, for Science itself can be neither good or evil, but its wrong use. If I may just touch here on your reference to machines, I would say that machines should not be allowed to mechanize human life but contribute to its well-being, which, as you rightly point out, it is constantly doing when it is man's sanity which controls the use of machinery.

Here, Rabindranath mentioned the efficacy of airplanes, continuing the idea used by Murray earlier. But what proves to be supremely important for our discussion of environmental degradation and the human cost of mechanization is Rabindranath's anticipation of an incident in world history that he was not to witness. He died in 1941 when the Second World War was ravaging the world. In 1945—a little more than a decade after Rabindranath wrote that letter to Murray, warning against the abuse of the power created through the use of science—the dropping of atom bombs on Hiroshima and Nagasaki at the end of the War meant the tragic beginning of a phase of civilization that continues to strike terror about the potential abuse of nuclear power and its suicidal consequences for mankind today. If man learns to exercise his moral power with discretion, and stops behaving in an imperious manner, then there would be a possibility of enjoying the products of the Machine Age for the benefit of mankind without being destructive.

It would appear that Rabindranath had this habit of homogenizing the West as abusive, but this was a practice that prevailed all over the world at that time, as is evident in Murray's description of the stereotypical behaviour of the East and the West. Rabindranath tried not to generalize and essentialize. It would be palpably facile to ignore the better side of the West and the worse parts of the East. Rabindranath critiqued the former in terms of habitual inhuman behaviour, the lack of self-appraisal and attempt to rectify past mistakes, and the unwillingness to learn the way to a harmonious coexistence of races and species, ensuring well-being for all. In *Raktakarabi*, he had already made his viewpoint clear in this regard. Moreover, at an earlier stage, his short story 'The Hidden Treasure' (1904) had also touched upon this idea. The issue is not primarily if modernity, science and technology are good or bad, but whether in the Machine Age, Rabindranath's attempts at upholding ecological harmony has any pertinence. An allegorical reading of 'The Hidden Treasure' might offer an answer.

'The Hidden Treasure' can be read as a criticism of the materialistic concern that prompts human beings to run after wealth thoughtlessly. It is a story in which one dehumanizes oneself so far as to think of committing murder for the sake of money. And yet this story indicates the necessity of simplicity and ecological harmony as the only means of survival. In this story, Mrityunjaya feels that he is entitled to power and riches. He has full faith in his family and cultural background. His family had been left untold riches and a puzzle as clue to its location, by a sage, generations ago. Mrityunjaya searched for this hidden treasure, moving far away from his home and undergoing great difficulty. He succeeded in solving the puzzle and felt that nothing could now stand between him and the treasure. But his ancestor Sankar, who had become a sanyasi, an ascetic wanderer, met him and declared that he had solved the puzzle earlier. Sankar advises Mrityunjaya not to covet the treasure for the wrong reasons, meaning that wealth and power should not be used for self-aggrandizement. Mrityunjaya needed to first understand his own nature, which was full of selfishness and covetousness. In the story, Sankar, as Mrityunjaya's ancestor, offered the wisdom and tradition of the past. Sankar tried to teach him the most precious lesson in, and of, life. Mrityunjaya was to learn, through pangs of hunger and thirst, and suffering through all the senses, that real treasure was not money and power, but the simple life in nature, found in the joy of the golden sunshine lying beyond his reach, as he starved in a cellar, sitting on a heap of gold that he could not even see in complete darkness. As in the Yaksha Puri in *Raktakarabi*, so in this story written earlier, gold is not shown to offer physical, emotional, aesthetic or spiritual succour. This treasure only emasculates and destroys life. In 'The Hidden Treasure,' Sankar told Mrityunjaya: 'That stone which you intended should kill me... has shattered forever the folly of my infatuation. Today I have seen how monstrous is the image of desire.'[35] Sankar was referring to his own search for the gold to alleviate the poverty of the younger generation of their family, and simultaneous attempt to assert his right over it. Mrityunjaya's attempt to murder Sankar for the treasure had made the older man conscious of the irrationality of greed. Yet Mrityunjaya continued to beg of Sankar: 'You are free, but I am not. I do not even want freedom. You must not cheat me of this wealth.'[36] The sanyasi then took him to the treasure[37]:

> On every side, thick plates of gold were arranged in piles. They stood against the walls glittering like heaped rays of solid sunlight stored in the bowels of the earth... Mrityunjaya [...] cried: 'All this gold is

mine—I will never part with it!'

'Very well,' replied the sannyasi, 'here is my torch, some barley and parched rice, and this large pitcher of water for you. Farewell.'

Sankar clanged the gigantic iron door shut on Mrityunjaya and the treasure, and left. All alone with the much-coveted treasure, Mrityunjaya felt ecstatic at the beginning. Rabindranath presents here a graphic description of the psychology of a person intoxicated with wealth[38]:

> Mrityunjaya began to go round and round the hall, touching the piles of gold again and again... When he woke, he saw the gold glittering on every side. There was nothing but gold. He began to wonder whether day had dawned and whether the birds were awake and revelling in the morning sunlight. It seemed as though in imagination he could smell the fragrant breeze of daybreak coming from the garden by the little lake near his home. It was as if he could actually see the ducks floating on the water, and hear their contented cackle as the maidservant came out from the house to the steps of the ghat, with the brass vessels in her hand, to be cleaned.

However, soon Mrityunjaya wanted to leave the dungeon. But he still could not bear to think of leaving all the gold behind. And the sanyasi refused to let him out so long as he retained vestiges of this greed. Mrityunjaya was locked alone with the gold in the dungeon for a longer stretch of time, and gradually he underwent a great psychological transformation portrayed with utmost sensitivity: 'He was seized with a longing to crush all these heaps of gold into dust and sweep them away with a broom. In this way, he could show his contempt for the covetous greed of all the kings and maharajahs of the world.'[39] He finally shouted for the sanyasi to open the door, saying that he did not want the gold[40]:

> But the door remained closed... He threw lump after lump of gold against it, but with no effect. Would the sanyasi leave him there to shrivel up and die, inch by inch, in that golden prison? As Mrityunjaya watched the gold, fear gripped him... [L]ayers of earth separated him from the most insignificant occurrences of life's varied and unceasing pilgrimage. That life, that sky, and that light appeared to him now as more priceless than all the treasures of the universe. He felt that if only he could, for one moment, again lie in the dusty lap of mother earth in her green-clad beauty, beneath the free open spaces of the sky, filling his lungs with the fragrant breeze laden with the scents of mown grass and of blossoms, he could die feeling that his life was complete.

It is after realizing—almost at the cost of his own life—the fact that the true wealth is life itself, that Mrityunjaya is permitted to come out of this prison of gold by Sankar. And when he is offered all the riches unconditionally, Mrityunjaya voluntarily throws away the only means to reach it.

Mrityunjaya may be considered to be an average man. His realization that the pursuit of wealth can be fatal can then teach a much-needed lesson in survival. The greedy, selfish individual or race can survive only when it keeps up with the rest of the world. Spontaneity, humility and love emerge as the three possible interrelated concepts that are necessary for the modern man's journey back to nature and survival. The alternative is to ignore the ethical side of the exploitation of nature due to greed, at one's own peril. In 'The Rule of the Giant' published in *Visva-Bharati Quarterly* in 1926, and delivered as lectures at the Dacca University and Andhra University, Rabindranath traced the process in which, in the name of modernization, man destroys nature and, consequently, himself, in a reminder of the first principle of ecology, which tells us that everything is related to everything else[41]:

> Today, there are vast stretches of desert on this earth where we see from the traces of dry river beds that once water flowed, trees flourished, rain fell, and that food was grown for cities now lying buried. It is evident that, with the complexity of living, through the disproportionate growth of non-life, the non-essential constantly extorted taxes from life, till life itself was made bankrupt by the extravagant egoism of man. There are invisible writings on the blank pages

of these desolate places which tell the story of how
some civilization had for ages elaborately busied itself
in preparing its own burial ground.

A number of things immediately draw our attention. Rabindranath evokes the basic principles of ecological and environmental sciences. This shows the repercussion of every bit of human action—like the felling a few trees at the local level—snowballing into major environmentally destructive practices at the global level. The history of the desert teaches us this lesson. The expansion of his vision from the local to the global in terms of the desertification means that Rabindranath, like any eminently practical environmental thinker in the twenty-first century society, was fully conscious of the links and passages among human, biotic and abiotic spheres. Disruptive activities in one part of the global ecosystem adversely affect not only that area, but also alter the face of the world for the worse. When he writes about 'the disproportionate growth of the non-essential', we understand that the path to proper environmental sustenance lies in getting our priorities right. And if our priorities include stopping environmental degradation and subsequent annihilation, then we have to assess the role played by Rabindranath himself at the micro-level of Santiniketan-Sriniketan. There he had to intervene emphatically to bring about a radical change in the environment of the place whose nature, ecology, economy and social fabric were well-nigh ruined when he had arrived there. He then took the decision to make a different kind of school, far away from the regimentation of thinking enforced in Calcutta and most of the cities in the modern world, where dissociation between nature and human life had already initiated a process of spiritual desertification.

NOTES

1. Tagore, *Man*, 51.
2. 'The Second Birth' *REW* 2: 377.
3. Ibid., 377.
4. Ibid., 377.
5. Ibid., 377.
6. Ibid., 377.
7. Ibid., 377–8.
8. Ibid., 378.
9. Ibid., 381.
10. Ibid., 378.
11. Ibid., 379.
12. Tagore, 'Hymn to the Tree,' 261–2.
13. Tagore, 'Subha,' 104.
14. Ibid., 105.
15. Ibid., 106.
16. Ibid., 108–9.
17. Tagore, 'Trespass,' 121.
18. Ibid., 122.
19. Ibid., 122–3.
20. Ibid., 123.

21. Ibid., 123.

22. Ibid., 124.

23. Ibid., 125.

24. Ibid., 125.

25. 'The Second Birth' *REW* 2: 379.

26. Ibid., 385.

27. Ibid., 386.

28. Tagore, *Gitanjali* Poem 14 *REW* 1: 47.

29. Tagore, *Gitanjali* Poem 36 *REW* 1: 53.

30. Tagore, *Gitanjali* Poem 73 *REW* 1: 68.

31. Gilbert Murray's letter in 'East and West' *REW* 3: 345–6.

32. Ibid., 346.

33. Ibid., 346.

34. Tagore's letter in 'East and West' *REW* 3: 347.

35. Tagore, 'The Hidden Treasure,' 130.

36. Ibid., 130.

37. Ibid., 132.

38. Ibid. 132.

39. Ibid., 133.

40. Ibid., 133–4.

41. Tagore, 'The Rule of the Giant' *REW* 3:576–7.

Chapter 5

Environmental Activism: Santiniketan-Sriniketan

We do not usually think of Rabindranath as an environmental activist. We are even less aware of the link between his ecophilosophy, institutional work at Santiniketan-Sriniketan and the literature written during this period, which reflected his experience there. In order to understand this, it is necessary to understand why he had to create a school in the lap of nature at Santiniketan in 1901. We get an indication of the relation among philosophy, environmental activism, the creation of an educational institution and his literary works from poem number 6 in *The Gardener* (1913)[1]:

> The tame bird was in the cage, the free bird was in the forest.
> They met when the time came, it was a decree of fate.
> The tree bird cries, 'O my love, let us fly to the wood.'
> The cage bird whispers, 'Come hither, let us both live

in the cage.'
Says the free bird, 'Among bars, where is there room
to spread one's wings?
'Alas,' cries the cage bird, 'I should not know where
to sit perched in the sky.'

In a mechanized age, the cage could well represent the one that man makes for himself with his material possessions. And then he does not want to venture beyond the comfort and security of that cage. The acquisitive spirit that takes man furthest from the freedom, the simple life and the beauty of nature becomes a habit and a convention. In the world of education too, Rabindranath knew well enough from his childhood experience that conventional schools were usually restrictive and repressive. They did not encourage the free flight of imagination and were unsupportive of a spirit that was not afraid to ask questions and seek knowledge on its own terms. In the world of both adult and young human beings then, questions of utility and quantifiable benefit create a cage. Beyond this, lies the freedom to soar high and far. But coming out of the cage is difficult for most of us. In poem 31 of *Gitanjali*, a somewhat similar situation had already been presented. It captures the nature of imprisonment that modern human beings devise for themselves, remarkably well[2]:

'Prisoner, tell me, who was it that bound you?'
    'It was my master,' said the prisoner. 'I thought
I could outdo everybody in the world in wealth and
power, and I amassed in my treasure-house the money

due to my King. When sleep overcame me I lay upon the bed that was for my lord, and on waking up I found I was a prisoner in my own treasure house.'

'Prisoner, tell me, who was it that wrought this unbreakable chain?'

'It was I,' said the prisoner, 'who forged this chain very carefully. I thought my invincible power would hold the world captive, leaving me in a freedom undisturbed. Thus, night and day, I worked at the chain with huge fires and cruel hard strokes. When at last the work was done and the links were complete and unbreakable, I found that it held me in its grip.'

The chain forged to keep the world in control, binds the greedy man instead. The image of the cage in the first poem, and the image of the manmade chain in the second, come together to signify the great deficiency found in the modern mechanized world that supplies all the necessary goods for human comfort and yet imprisons us. It is significant that human beings yearn for freedom. This freedom would signify an existence that is natural, and where one is satisfied in not having an overtly mechanical way of life and thought.

In essay number 106 from *Thoughts from Tagore* (1921), the images used in the poems above take a concrete shape. Rabindranath makes a statement, signifying the disjunction between a modern, mechanized world and the simple, calm life of nature[3]:

In our highly complex modern civilization, mechanical forces are organized with such efficiency that the materials produced grow far in advance of man's selective and assimilative capacity to simplify them into harmony, with his nature and needs. Such an intemperate overgrowth of things, like the rank vegetation of the tropics, creates confinement for man. The nest is simple, it has an easy relationship with the sky; the cage is complex and costly, it is too much itself, excommunicating whatever lies outside. And modern man is busy building his cage, fast developing his parasitism on the monster, Thing, which he allows to envelop him on all sides. He is always occupied in adapting himself to its dead angularities, limits himself to its limitations, and merely becomes part of it.

The distinction between a free existence in nature in the past and the artificial comfort of civilization in the modern era has its parallel in the images of the nest and the cage.

In *Talks in China*, Rabindranath asked an important question: 'Why should there remain, for ever, a gulf between progress and perfection? [...] It is your mission to prove that love for the earth, and for the things of the earth, is possible without materialism,—love without a strain of greed.'[4] In other words, progress in the modern world should mean harmonious and sustainable development, not consuming so indiscriminately that everything is destroyed soon. In addition, we learn from Section 108 of *Thoughts from Tagore* that 'All civilizations are creations. They do not merely offer us information about themselves, but give outer expression to some inner ideals which are creative. Therefore we judge each civilization, not by how much it has produced, but by what idea it expresses in its activities.'[5] Rabindranath's designation of a civilization as creation instead of construction or mere accumulation of possessions removes it from the domain of mechanical and restrictive practices. It envisages growth with freedom, unity, harmony and joy. He tried to uphold the values of a civilization that would serve both man and nature with humility, simplicity and love. It is in this context that his work at Santiniketan-Sriniketan becomes significant as active environmental intervention, and the literature reflecting his eco-conscious ideas during this period remains pioneering.

It is a well-known fact that Rabindranath, since the days of his childhood, had always found the schools he had attended and the contemporary curriculum, quite stifling. If anything, the educational programme prevailing in India in the nineteenth century, was, at the most, meant to create a series of babus, who would work for the British ruler gratefully. In contrast, for the children of his son Rathindranath's generation, Rabindranath wanted something unique by Indian standards in those days. He wanted to nurture a child in such a manner that, later, a worthy person would come into being. It was for this purpose that he had decided to set up a school at Santiniketan.

A place near Bolpur, in the district of Birbhum, in the

arid, western part of undivided Bengal, had been chosen by Maharshi Debendranath Tagore, Rabindranath's father, as an ashram—an abode of peace, meditation and communion with God. It did not have the privilege of being well-connected to Calcutta. It was not even at a place where the usual greenery characterizing Bengal would make everything picturesque. It contained villagers whose energy had been depleted by attacks of malaria and other diseases amidst grinding poverty and appalling ignorance. Further, it was a totally rustic and tribal place where the famed culture of the Jorasanko Tagore family could not be expected to flourish. But still, Debendranath and Rabindranath—father and son—had successively chosen it as the place where they could taste a fuller life. Maharshi Debendranath had named this place Santiniketan. Rabindranath, in 1901, had established a Brahmacharyashram there, with five boys in residence. In a boarding school far away from Calcutta, with rudimentary facilities for living and studying, he sought—without much experience—to inculcate the values that were most essential to learning fully about oneself as a human being in the scheme of life on earth.

Santiniketan was not a new place to Rabindranath. Although the ashram was established in 1863, he first visited the place at the age of twelve with his father, in 1873[6]:

> ...when he was a mere boy and was very much fascinated by its placid beauty, its blue and boundless sky, its limitless horizon and its palm trees lined up

in the lap of the nature. Little did he know that the place would be known the world over as the centre of his highest creative achievement. Debendranath had already built there a prayer hall—a Brahmo temple... open to the light and air on all sides... as far back as 1891. This time in September 1901, he came to Santiniketan with his family at the age of forty, with the approval of his father, and the Santiniketan Brahmavidyalaya was founded on 22 December [...] of the same year.

Santiniketan did not have any infrastructure so to say, not even for setting up a tiny institution like the Brahmacharyashram. In his own innovative way, turning a gaping deficiency into an opportunity for empathy with natural life, Rabindranath singlehandedly altered the face of the place for the better. Possibly, what had attracted him to this place was not only the provision made in the Trust Deed of 1887 regarding the Santiniketan Ashram created by Debendranath for the establishment of a Brahmavidyalaya, but, at a more basic level, the place itself, with its open fields stretching to the horizon on all sides. The very sight of this open space and the free and full play of colours in the sky would help the mind, imagination and spirit to expand marvellously, especially when compared to his experience in Calcutta as a schoolboy.

Rabindranath had intended to create, at Santiniketan, an environment that would bring nature and culture together, thereby creating an opportunity to learn directly about life in the context of the world[7]:

> ...man's introduction to this world is his introduction to his final truth in a simple form. He is born into a world which to him is intensely living, where he as an individual occupies the full attention of his surroundings. Then he grows up to doubt this deeply personal aspect of reality, he loses himself in the complexity of things, separates himself from his surroundings, often in spirit of antagonism. But this shattering of the unity of truth, this uncompromising civil war between his personality and his outer world, can never find its meaning in interminable discord. Thereupon to find the true conclusion of his life, he has to come back through this digression of doubt to the simplicity of perfect truth, to his union with all in an infinite bond of love.
>
> ...The young mind should be saturated with the idea that it has been born in a human world which is in harmony with the world around it...The highest education is that which does not merely give us information but makes our life in harmony with all existence.

This is the reason why he had created an institution where the students would sit under trees and learn as much from the lessons written in books and taught by teachers as the natural environment surrounding them.

Today, more than a hundred years after the tiny school at Santiniketan had been created, tourists from different parts of Bengal, India as well as the world, arrive to wonder at the tradition of Rabindranath's time still being followed at Santiniketan. The students of the Patha Bhavana, or secondary school, continue to study at the ashrama, sitting in the open, with the trees offering them shade. Some think of this as quaint; others wonder at this sight on the campus of a Central University, and—as from the very beginning—there are yet others, including great figures in the world of culture and education, who remain quite sceptical about the efficacy of the practice. But if we are trying to understand Santiniketan, we have to remember and carefully analyse exactly how and why Rabindranath had sought to create it in this unique manner.

In Santiniketan, Rabindranath wanted to offer a nest to the students, not a cage (gilded or otherwise). The students would taste natural life fully. But they would not taste luxury at this formative, impressionable stage. In terms of material possessions and comfort, Rabindranath had very little to offer to the students at Santiniketan for many years. Paucity of funds was, however, just one part of the story. The real reason behind the poverty of the ashram and its residents was Rabindranath's belief that simplicity was the key to the best possible life, free from want and greed, creating and fostering the perfect environment for the all-round development of mind and body[8]:

None of ... [the] basic requirements existed at that time. C.F. Andrews, who came to Santiniketan thirteen years after the foundation of the school, did not notice any change in the situation. He wrote [...] the school was comparatively small and the buildings were few and far between. The mango grove itself was the chief place for lessons and when it rained we went into the dormitories and sat on the sides of the cots. In fact, the Santiniketan Bari was the only brick-built house in those days. Teachers and students lived in the Adi Kutir—a mud house. According to the Trust Deed of Maharshi, no one could live permanently in the Santiniketan Bari with family. Rabindranath, therefore, had to acquire 20 bighas of land and construct houses for the use of the Ashram school...

In the words of Rathindranath Tagore: 'In spite of everything—all the poverty and want, the lack of every comfort and convenience—nobody complained because we really believed in simple living and took pride in our poverty.'

If we remember that Rathindranath was not only Rabindranath's son but also one of the first students of the school at Santiniketan, then his words bear witness to the fact that from the very beginning, Santiniketan was not only a place—it represented something much more than that. Visva-Bharati has the motto *'Yatra visva bhavatyekanidam'*, signifying where the world makes a home in a single nest with its origin in Rabindranath's school. This represents a concept, a particular world view, and a philosophy. Part of this philosophy, Rabindranath repeatedly declared, was derived from the idea of the Gurukul ashrams in ancient India where students from everywhere would congregate in search of knowledge, and part of it was in keeping with his idea of giving a child the freedom and scope to explore the world on his own and learn from it. This is what Rabindranath had tried to fashion Santiniketan as: not just a school, a location prized for helping him meditate, or a picturesque place, but an opportunity for the self to harmonize itself with the other, or the whole world awaiting assimilation with the individual consciousness[9]:

> We have come to this world to accept it, not merely to know it… From our very childhood, habits are formed and knowledge is imparted in such a manner that our life is weaned away from nature and our mind and the world are set in opposition from the beginning of our days… We rob the child of his earth to teach him geography… I well remember the surprise and annoyance of an experienced headmaster, reputed to be a successful disciplinarian, when he saw one of the boys of my school climbing a tree and choosing a fork of the branches for settling down to his studies… What is surprising is to notice the same headmaster's approbation of the boy's studying botany. He believes in an impersonal knowledge of the tree because it is

science, but not in a personal experience of it. This
growth of experience leads to forming instinct, which
is the result of nature's own method of instruction... I
myself was brought up in a cultured home in a town,
and as far as my personal behaviour goes, I have been
obliged to act all through my life as if I were born
in a world where there are no trees.

Therefore, I consider it as a part of education for
my boys to let them fully realize that they are in a
scheme of existence where trees are a substantial fact,
not merely as generating chlorophyll and taking carbon
from the air, but as living trees.

Santiniketan continues to exist today as a popular tourist destination, an Indian heritage site and by virtue of Visva-Bharati, a Central University—as an institution of education at all levels. But how far is it Rabindranath's Santiniketan? The place had been bare. The very openness of the country that had been so attractive to the poet initially also meant that there were scarcely any trees, any habitation from one end of the horizon to the other. It had been, literally as well as metaphorically, his canvas. Rabindranath had filled it in with green, first informally, and later, through the tree-planting festival, Briksharopan, which he had instituted at the ashram on 14 July 1928. He composed, for the students and the ashramites, on that occasion, a story called 'Balai', celebrating the bond between the natural world and humans. In this way, he literally defined and refashioned the place and its culture. This was a far cry from the way it had been when Rabindranath had initially experienced it[10]:

> All round our ashram is a vast open country, bare up to the line of the horizon except for sparsely growing stunted date palms and prickly shrubs struggling with anthills. Below the level of the field, there extend numberless mounds and tiny hillocks of red gravel... intersected by narrow channels of rainwater... A road used by the village people... goes meandering through the lonely fields, with its red dust staring in the sun...

To Rabindranath, Santiniketan never was a laboratory for experimenting with an alternative system of education and culture. To him, it was a dream or rather a concept. He had explained his intentions clearly when he stated[11]:

> I am an artist and not a man of science, and, therefore, my institution necessarily has assumed the aspect of a work of art and not that of a pedagogical laboratory... From the commencement of our work, we have encouraged our children to be of service to our neighbours from which has grown up a village reconstruction work in our neighbourhood, unique in the whole of India. Round our educational work, the villages have grouped themselves, in which the sympathy for nature and service for man have become one. In such an extension of sympathy and service, our mind realizes its true freedom.

Thus, Sriniketan and the rural reconstruction work based there, had come into being to complement the poet's effort in Santiniketan. They were combined within Visva-Bharati to balance the poetic and cultural with the practical and scientific, in an effort to bring together the best of modern Western knowledge with the best in the East. Not only tradition and modernity, and past and present, but also the local and the universal were, thus, expected to come together at Rabindranath's Santiniketan, which was meant to represent the wholeness of life.

Rabindranath, in his work on ecology, had had certain distinguished collaborators from an early phase. Biophysicist Jagadish Chandra Bose, another great Indian, was one of the earliest in the world to scientifically establish facts about plant life, the nature of the relationship between external stimulus and the reaction of living entities, and the relation between biotic and abiotic components in an ecology. As an author himself, with a sensitive aesthetic sense, he was one who appreciated Rabindranath's literary and welfare work and remained a friend and correspondent always. Another was Patrick Geddes (1854–1932), a famous biologist, environmentalist and regional planner from Scotland who had written the biography of Jagadish Chandra Bose and been a friend to Rabindranath. This was a fortunate union. Patrick Geddes was the founder of the Environment Society in 1884 and worked on environmental activism for long in terms of the Land-People-Environment movement.[12] As a mark of their friendship and collaboration, his son Arthur

Geddes (1895–1968), a specialist in human geography and social engineering, became a disciple of Rabindranath since 1921. The Geddes' appreciation of, and association with Rabindranath marks their intimate knowledge of and regard for Santiniketan as well.

For Rabindranath, Santiniketan or the 'abode of peace' was the place that he decided to live in. One can be a temporary, yet appreciative visitor to a place. The alternative is to stay in one's native place. It is a rare category to which Rabindranath belongs. He chose as his centre of work and residence, a new and inhospitable place[13]:

> The unalienated lover of nature inhabits; the alienated lover of nature gazes. The first is a native, deeply embedded in a stable ecosystem; the second is a Romantic, a tourist, a newcomer... The conventional assumption is that the transition from preindustrial to industrial society abolishes the first and engenders the second... Environmentalists hope it may be possible to break the sequence in which estrangement from nature is followed by Romantic regret and desire. They believe in the possibility of sustainable forms of development that will not estrange communities from their natural environments... Environmentalists seek to build alliance between tourist and native, hoping for an eventual society in which everyone will move between these positions.

Rabindranath was not born in Santiniketan. Yet, like a native, he sought to create and inhabit a stable ecology in the place. He goes beyond the issue of a place affecting a person and prompts us to appreciate the effect of the person as the dream-creation of the place. For Rabindranath[14]:

> the growth of this school was the growth of my life...
> The trees seemed to me like silent hymns rising from the mute heart of the earth, and the shouts and laughter of the boys mingling in the evening sky came before me like trees of living sounds rising up from the depth of human life. I found my message in the sunlight that touched my inner mind and felt a fullness in the sky that spoke to me in the word of our ancient rishi... 'Who could ever move and strive and live in this world if the sky were not filled with love?'

The natural environment represented by the trees is complemented by the cultural environment created by the spontaneous activities of the children at the school. But it must be remembered that Santiniketan, at the time of its origin, had been just a 'vast open country, bare up to the line of the horizon except for sparsely growing stunted date palms and prickly shrubs'.[15] In other words, it was due to his own love for the place that Rabindranath created a particular natural and cultural environment there. It is for this reason that he sought to teach the students at Santiniketan the message of integration of the vast intellectual space spread all over the world with the homely place at Birbhum whose natural environment he was adorning with trees, in loving care. Hence, he had initiated Briksharopan, or the tree-planting ceremony, and the Halakarshan, or the symbolical tilling of the land to augment cultivation. It is a reflection of the knowledge derived from the rapidly growing fields of agricultural science and technology in the Western countries that was to be found in Rabindranath's introduction of the tractor at Sriniketan. Thus, knowledge derived from the burgeoning space of different types of research in other parts of the world was brought to use to make life better at Santiniketan-Sriniketan, the chosen homeplace. Taken together, all these activities served as a potent inspiration to creative work as well. In other words, we may say that the loving work at Santiniketan-Sriniketan had offered the scope for the creative space that Rabindranath needed to compose his songs and to write and paint. Ecology signifies the process that governs the relationship between organisms and their environment. In his place-based work ethics, Rabindranath created and sustained an ecology that brought together the best from the wider space of the world to nourish the homely place at Santiniketan. '"Dwelling" is not a transient state; rather, it implies the long-term imbrication of humans in a landscape of memory, ancestry and death, of ritual, life and work.'[16]

Rabindranath's attempts to initiate changes, for the better, in the environment and ecology of Santiniketan was not an ordinary desire to sustain the home. One seeks to make a positive difference to one's place of birth. He sought to usher changes, inspired equally by the ancient Vedic knowledge regarding the harmonious living of all and the most modern research in the West, to make, not the place of his birth, but the place he had adopted more homelike to everybody, at Santiniketan-Sriniketan. This inspires one to expand the meaning of the *local*ity of one's homeplace to link it with the idea of the earthly 'home', habitat or oikos, in terms of an all-pervasive love for the integrally interrelated and harmonious coexistence of all life forms in its ecology. It is the kind of existential philosophy based on love, care and work for all, in turn, that bears testimony to the expansive nature of the mental 'space' that Rabindranath had had. The process had started long ago at Shilaidaha, to bring the best knowledge from the urban world to improve the condition of the ecology in the humble, rural homeplace. It found its culmination, quite logically, in Santiniketan. The expansive space of his thoughts and dreams came to be reflected here[17]:

> I was brought up in an atmosphere of aspiration, aspiration for the expansion of the human spirit. We in our home sought freedom of power in our language, freedom of imagination in our literature, freedom of soul in our religious creeds and that of mind in our social environment. Such an opportunity has given me confidence in the power of education, which is one with life and which only can give us real freedom, the highest that is claimed for man, his freedom of

moral communion in the human world... I try to assert in my words and works that education has its only meaning and object in freedom—freedom from ignorance about the laws of the universe, and freedom from passion and prejudice in our communication with the human world. In my institution, I have attempted to create an atmosphere of naturalness in our relationship with strangers, and the spirit of hospitality, which is the first virtue in men that made civilization possible.

The world, according to Rabindranath, then, was just as much welcome to his home as this humble home was to feel free to be at one with the world beyond. The Nobel Prize turned him into a world citizen[18]:

Henceforth, he was more a world citizen than an Indian. He was a world citizen not because he became world famous but because he felt with the world... Tagore made the world's destiny his own and felt deeply the agony if there was suffering and injustice in any part of the world. This world consciousness [...] was very real in him...

Feeling at one with the world—the one immediately around him in the poor, illiterate villages of Bengal as well as the one that spread over distant shores, telling him other narratives of suffering and deprivation—Rabindranath could yet not feel at home in it, given his experience of the magnitude of anguish everywhere. Yet again, in the whole corpus of his poems and songs, what becomes evident is an intense love for both the natural and the human domain, in terms of real place and imaginative space. This love felt at home in the world, in the most comprehensive sense. If we now remember the idea of Rabindranath's repeated voyages in the universal cultural and intellectual space, and subsequent return to the homeplace of Santiniketan, then a new significance emerges from the analysis of his thoughts about the home and the world. From a stage where he would not feel at home in a world full of suffering, there appeared to be a movement towards a stage in which he sought to bring the world together by means of apposite education and culture—in Santiniketan—to preserve through love and a proper understanding of life—civilization itself—aspiring to create a home for it, there. Even more significantly, he sought to bring together the human and the natural spheres, in his concept of a true civilization, as the basis of this enterprise. This added another dimension to his 'being' at home in the world—in that the real world is earth, or oikos. Therefore, as part of the civilizing and educational enterprise, when Rabindranath initiated the tree-planting festival at Santiniketan on 14 July 1928, he read out a short story, 'Balai,' composed for the occasion. It is this story that epitomizes Rabindranath's innermost feeling about being at home in the world[19]:

> Although written for an occasion, 'Balai' is not an occasional story: it reflects a lifelong trait of the

author's sensibility. Already in 1892, he had written in a
letter to Indira Debi Choudharani: 'I clearly remember
how many ages ago, when the maiden earth looked up
from her sea-bath and worshipped the stripling sun,
I, on the fresh soil of that young earth, was bursting
into life like a tree in some primal energy of vitality.'

In 'Balai', the boy seemed to be at one with the clouds, the rain, the forest, the grass and each little nameless plant. The silk-cotton tree that he had chosen to be his 'life's friend' at his childhood homeplace, had continued to grow—in his imagination—with himself, even as he was being trained at Shimla first, with the prospect of relocating to London, to explore a larger intellectual space, soon after.[20] The image of the tree represented home life to the exiled Balai and he continued to commune with the natural world: 'Balai could read that eternal message of life in his bloodstream.'[21] The cutting down of each plant, however insignificant, by an adult, would wound him deeply and he would watch helplessly, as the world would appear to be less secure, less homelike, to him. Balai, like the author himself, had gone out into the wide world and yet, had continued to foster an unaffected sentiment for homely life, making the whole earth his own in loving care for even the most insignificant manifestation of life. It is this care that Rabindranath lavished on places he adopted, Santiniketan being the greatest manifestation of positive environmental intervention, his loving creation.

NOTES

1. Tagore, *The Gardener* Poem 6 *REW* 1:85.
2. Tagore, *Gitanjali* Poem 31 *REW* 1:52.
3. *Thoughts from Tagore* Section 106 *REW* 3:58–59.
4. Tagore, 'Talks in China' *REW* 2:608.
5. *Thoughts from Tagore* Section 108 *REW* 3: 59.
6. Neogy, *The Twin Dreams of Rabindranath Tagore: Santiniketan and Sriniketan*, 5–6.
7. Tagore, 'My School' *REW* 2:389–90.
8. Neogy, *The Twin Dreams of Rabindranath Tagore: Santiniketan and Sriniketan*, 8–9.
9. Tagore, 'My School,' *REW* 2:390–2.
10. Ibid., 396.
11. Tagore, 'The Educational Mission of Visva-Bharati,' *REW* 3:627.
12. Banerjee, *Tagore and Geddes*, 16.
13. Kerridge, 'Ecological Hardy,' 134.
14. Tagore, 'My School,' *REW* 2:397.
15. Ibid., 396.
16. Garrard, *Ecocriticism*, 108.
17. Tagore, 'Ideals of Education,' 286–7.
18. Kripalani, *Rabindranath Tagore: A Biography*, 267.
19. Ghosh, T. Introduction tr. Sukanta Chaudhuri. *Rabindranath Tagore: Selected Short Stories*, 27–28.
20. Tagore, 'Balai,' 259.
21. Ibid., 257.

Conclusion

In Santiniketan-Sriniketan, Rabindranath's attempt was to integrate through the students, human life with natural existence in such a manner that both would flourish. However, the situation at Santiniketan-Sriniketan was extremely inhospitable at the beginning[1]:

> A journey through the district of Birbhum will show even to the casual observer that all is not well. The press is constantly giving you statistics showing the increasing death rate, the all powerful sway of malaria and disease, the grinding poverty and the frequency of famine in this area... You may object that the district is notorious for its poor soil... But in this, history is against you. The Birbhum area was once the richest district of Bengal, and supported upon the cultivation of the soil a large and flourishing community.

It is this degraded soil and backward, underdeveloped area that Rabindranath had deliberately chosen to work on. As in his positive environmental and cultural intervention here, so in his literary works we see a reflection of the ideals of humility, love and service. It was a world of a unified existence of nature and culture that Rabindranath wanted to establish at the microcosmic, local level, at Santiniketan-Sriniketan. Santiniketan gradually established itself as the centre of education and culture in the tree-lined locality that was emerging according to Rabindranath's vision. If Santiniketan had been a barren, empty field earlier, Sriniketan was located among moribund villages that had forgotten the life-sustaining abilities of the rural community. Rabindranath's diligent work with villagers in Shelidah, Patisar, Kaligram and other places within the Tagore family estate, since the 1890s, inspired him to think of the resuscitation of the village communities lying so close to his beloved Santiniketan. The efforts of the Tagore family, and Elmhirst, along with that of the volunteers from the Santiniketan community contributed in a major way towards the amalgamation of fragmented, tiny landholdings in villages in Sriniketan. Rabindranath's efforts were to increase agricultural productivity and improve the peasants' condition, without any thought to the expenses—material and physical—incurred in the process. The introduction of the tractor, where necessary, suggests that his view of science and technology was never backward. It also suggests that to reclaim nature in Sriniketan—degraded through prolonged neglect, exploitation and abuse, as evaluated by Elmhirst—Rabindranath remained receptive of the fruits of contemporary advancement in various areas of life. So he exhorted the local peasants to cultivate subsidiary crops to supplement the main crop, and encouraged earth-based cottage industries like pottery, even contributing his Nobel prize money to an agricultural bank that would eventually help Sriniketan. His concern was about the sustenance of not only the intellectual but also the rural community in Santiniketan-Sriniketan. This was reflected in the practical implementation of his ideals of a holistic nurture of nature and culture simultaneously. The scale of operation, perforce, had to remain limited to his property and the family estate in Sriniketan and Santiniketan respectively, just as earlier, his plans for the rural compatriots could be implemented in the vicinity of Kaligram. His travels and thoughts continued to encompass worldwide concerns throughout the period, in terms of an ever-widening intellectual space. These thoughts and activities were not reflecting the 'mere words of a poet or empty exhortations of a patriot-politician… [but of] a man who had already practiced to the full what he now preached.'[2]

In case Rabindranath thought of preaching anything, it was just one thing—that the world should never move along a brutal, destructive and suicidal path. As an indictment of prevalent global practices, he wrote: 'Power in the animals was, at least, in harmony with life, but not so are bombs, poison gases, and murderous aeroplanes, the horrible weapons supplied by science.'[3] This is why he had to issue a warning against all forms of exploitation, in the human as well as the natural world in a near-scriptural language[4]:

> What is the value of success if it be at the cost of humanity and if it make a desert of God's world?... We need to hear this again and again and never more than now in this modern world of slavery and cannibalism in decent guise: By the help of unrighteousness, men do prosper, men do gain victories over their enemies, men do attain what they desire; but they perish at the root.

He issued this warning repeatedly. While introducing Elmhirst's speech, as 'The Robbery of the Soil,' he made the idea of such suicide vivid[5]:

> I often imagine that the moon [...] produced the condition for life to be born on her soil earlier than was possible on [earth]. Once [...] her storehouse was perpetually replenished with food for her children. Then in the course of time some race was born to her [...] that began greedily to devour its own surroundings... their career of plunder entirely outstripped nature's power for recuperation... At last one day, the moon, like a fruit whose pulp had been completely eaten by the insects which it had sheltered, became a hollow shell, a universal grave... In other words, they behaved exactly in the way human beings of today are behaving upon this earth, fast exhausting their store of sustenance, not because they must live

> their normal life, but because they must live at a pitch
> of monstrous excess.

However, it is not for his words as a prophet of doom that his appeal as an environmental thinker remains extant. His work at Santiniketan-Sriniketan, though not existing in exactly the same form at present, stands as testimony to the extent of his advanced environmental and educational thought and practice.

Let us turn to the question about Santiniketan today. In case we want to criticize Rabindranath's inability to create a self-sustaining place at Santiniketan, then what do we find? On the one hand, it will be argued that there has been modernization, urbanization and extension of civic facilities throughout the place and this is quite natural, in keeping with the exigencies of our times. Rabindranath himself was never averse to keeping pace with the changing times. On the other hand, it might be argued that Santiniketan has now become a commercialized version of its former self. The simplicity as well as grandeur of Rabindranath's vision is lost, given the daily insurgence of numerous tourists. However, there might again exist a third point of view that Visva-Bharati, through the rural reconstruction work at the villages it had adopted for the purpose, the universally esteemed work at Kala Bhavana and the celebration of the Briksharopan, Halakarshan and season-based festivals like Basantotsav initiated by Rabindranath, among other instances, continues to keep Santiniketan unique, not only in respect of Indian education, but in the whole world. Visva-Bharati continues to uphold Rabindranath's ideals. For instance, this is the place where the tree-planting ceremony is still held[6]:

> Tagore's Santiniketan is neither Shakespeare's Stratford, Voltaire's Ferney or Thoreau's Concord, but a curious cocktail of all these... Today, visiting Santiniketan, one is aware of confusion. The place seems to be in a cusp of two cultures; between the pulse of an [sic] university and the trappings of a memorial... What survives till today amid all the confusion and conflict is the spirit of redemption... On my way back to the station, I met a young boy, incandescent in his ochre uniform. I asked his name and the class he studied. And then inquired, for whom was he carrying the small sapling? He replied with determination and a little diffidence, 'I will plant it outside my window today. Every year I do.'

Rabindranath's legacy survives. But what constitutes this legacy? Is it to be found in the script of life that he wrote in literature? Or, does it lie in the life he wrote on the land in remote parts of Bengal? Or, perhaps, this legacy covers the life and the land together? This legacy covers the places of the world he was a sojourner of. It covers, possibly, an entire life dedicated to loving nature. Hence, in the last few months of his life, he looked back at his childhood and brought together the beginning with the end, soon to come[7]:

Called 'Sahitye Aitihasikata'—'Historicality in Literature' would be a fair translation—it is the last article but one of Tagore's prose writings… Dated May 1941, it is an authorized transcription of his comments made in the course of a dialogue… For the death of the poet, some ten weeks later in August that year, makes it one of the very last things he had to say on the subject.

The subject was Rabindranath recounting childhood memories. He commented on the process of gathering experiences and reading, which would be fashioned into literature later. Rabindranath described this to his interviewer, the Bengali poet Buddhadev Basu. He contrasted this memory with the records in a book of history. He felt that the emergence of the poetic self is not recorded in the pages of history books as we know them, but is essential to the poet himself[8]:

> I find it difficult to put up with the pedantic historian when he tries to force me out of the center of my creativity as a poet. Let us go back to the inaugural moment of my poetical career… It's a daybreak in winter. A pale light is beginning to filter through the darkness… Like everybody else, I too, could have stayed happily curled up in bed until at least six in the morning. But it was not possible for me to do so. There was a garden within the inner precincts of our house. Indigent like myself, all it had for its wealth

> was mostly a row of coconut trees lining the eastern wall. Yet I used to be in such a hurry lest I should miss anything of what I saw every day as the light fell on the trembling coconut fronds and the dewdrops burst into glitter. I used to think that this joy of the welcoming dawn would be of interest to all the other boys as well... But as I grew older I came to realize that there was no other child nearly so keen to see the light vibrating on shrubs and trees... There's nothing in it that comes out of the mold of history... It is precisely in this that one is a poet. One day I had just come back from school at about four-thirty and found a dark blue cumulus suspended high above the third storey of our house. What a marvelous sight that was. Even now I remember that day. But in the history of that day there was no one other than myself who saw those clouds in quite the same way as I did or was similarly thrilled. Rabindranath happened to be all by himself in that instance.

Rabindranath describes those moments of his childhood memory that he remembered vividly to the end of his life. He had not started writing poetry at that early stage of his life. It is in hindsight as a mature poet, then, that he realized the potentially poetical nature of his childhood sights. The memory of the emergence of the distinct poetic self is carefully distinguished from mundane history by Rabindranath in this description. However, of greater critical significance is the following segment of his statement, especially in the context of the way in which he distinguishes the history of Rabindranath as a mere subject in India under British rule, and the singular self that had an inner existence[9]:

> Once after school I saw a most amazing spectacle from our western verandah. A donkey—not one of those donkeys manufactured by British imperial policy but the animal [...] had come up from the washermen's quarters and was grazing on the grass while a cow fondly licked its body. The attraction of one living being for another that then caught my eye has remained unforgettable for me until today... This I know for certain. No one else was instructed by the history of that day in the profound significance of the sight as was Rabindranath. In his own field of creativity, Rabindranath has been entirely alone and tied to no public by history. Where history was public, he was there merely as a British subject but not as Rabindranath himself. The bizarre game of political change was being played out there, of course, but the light that glittered on the foliage of coconut palms was not a statist input owing to the British government. It radiated within some mysterious history of my inner soul and manifested itself in its own blissful form every day in various ways. As it has been said in our Upanishads: 'It is not for the sake of the sons, my dear, that they are loved, but for one's own sake

that they are loved.' The atma wishes to manifest itself as the creator in its love for its son. That is why it values its love for the son so much. The creator gathers some of the material for his creation from historical narratives and some from his social environment. But the material by itself does not make him a creator. It is only by putting it to use that he expresses himself as the creator… I have not been able to put the entire history of my life in words, but that history is of no importance. It is the desire for self-expression on the part of man as the creator, that has engaged him in all his long endeavors over the ages. Try and highlight only the history which is piloted by man-as-creator towards the Magnum that lies beyond history and is at the very center of the human soul. This was known to our Upanishads. The message the Upanishads have for me is what I have taken from them on my own initiative. That stands for an agenthood which is mine alone.

As Rabindranath emphasized, neither the chronological history of each and every moment of his life, nor the vicissitudes in the career of the nations, matter so much as a recounting of those moments of his life—those incidents in his world of thought and work—that reveal the centre of his soul. In an ecobiography, too, it is a carefully scripted version of the moments of ecological 'agenthood' that matters. The outcome of such moments, with the individual acting for the sustenance of ecological harmony, might have various degrees of success or failure. It is the attempt that counts in the ecobiography, as does the spirit that inspires, informs and fosters the work. For Rabindranath, this lifelong work to harmonize God, nature and the human world was the unfolding of his poetic self. Rabindranath, the creator of Visva-Bharati, is in the same sense the poet who must sing of nature and God's glory in this world. It is perhaps fitting that the poet of harmony in life and nature is paid an ecobiographical tribute with his own song[10]:

> My heart sings at the wonder of my place
> in this world of light and life;
> at the feel in my pulse of the rhythm of
>   creation
> cadenced by the swing of the endless time.

> I feel the tenderness of the grass in my
>   forest walk,
> the wayside flowers startle me:
> that the gifts of the infinite are strewn
>   in the dust
> wakens my son in wonder.

> I have seen, have heard, have lived;
> in the depth of the known have felt
> the truth that exceeds all knowledge
> which fills my heart with wonder and
>   I sing.

NOTES

1. Leonard Knight Elmhirst delivered a lecture 'The Robbery of the Soil' on 28 July 1922 under the auspices of the Visva-Bharati Sammilani and published it in *The Modern Review* in October 1922. It became a part of his book: *Poet and Plowman* 27.
2. Kripalani, *Rabindranath Tagore: Biography* 162.
3. Tagore, 'Talks in China,' *REW* 2:605.
4. Ibid., 602.
5. Rabindranath Tagore introduced Elmhirst's ideas in 'Robbery of the Soil'.
   Tagore, 'Robbery of the Soil' in *Poet and Plowman* 22–23.
6. Datta, 'Festival of the Earth.'
7. Tagore, 'Historicality in Literature,' 76.
8. Ibid., 96–97.
9. Ibid., 97–99.
10. Tagore, Poem 67, *Poems*, 101.

Acknowledgements

During 2010–11, this book started taking shape in the course of my Post-Doctoral Fellowship at Rabindranath Tagore Centre for Human Development Studies (sponsored by the University Grants Commission), a joint initiative of the Calcutta University and the Institute of Development Studies, Kolkata. Professor Amiya Kumar Bagchi was the coordinator of the Centre at the time. This great economist was also my strictest and most learned interlocutor on Tagore during the writing of the book. I take this occasion to pay homage to Professor Jasodhara Bagchi who, from time to time, permitted me to derive benefit from her observations on Tagore and ecofeminism. Gayatri Chakravorty Spivak, an institution by herself, cajoled me repeatedly to extend my critical horizons by asking persistently why Tagore merits an ecocritical reading today, and read the first draft of my report on this subject. All other colleagues, academic and non-academic, at Rabindranath Tagore Centre for Human Development Studies, provided all sorts of support ungrudgingly. Visva-Bharati is my original workplace and my senior colleagues there continue to exhort me to excel. My teacher, Professor Jharna Sanyal of Calcutta University has always encouraged my efforts. So also has Professor Sanjukta Dasgupta.

The book could not have been written without the help of the library staff of Rabindranath Tagore Centre for Human Development Studies, the British Council Library, Kolkata, the National Library and the libraries in Visva-Bharati.

I have quoted, with gratitude, sections on and from *Gitanjali*, *The Waterfall*, *Red Oleanders* and a few essays and lectures by Tagore from the monumental four-volume *English Writings of Rabindranath Tagore*, a Sahitya Akademi publication.

The officials at the Rabindra-Bhavana photo archives of Visva-Bharati have kindly given me the permission to use the beautiful photograph of Rabindranath Tagore looking at nature outside from his room, towards the end of his life, for this volume.

Dibakar Ghosh, Jyotsna Mehta and Debangana Banerjee of Rupa have helped me, with utmost patience, to give shape to this volume.

My parents, my husband and my son have made a lot of sacrifices to make it possible for me to write this book.

I am grateful to each of them.

Bibliography

Alam, Fakrul and Radha Chakravarty ed. *The Essential Tagore* (Kolkata: Visva-Bharati, 2011).

Aruna, Marie Josephine. "Letters' and Ecopoetics.' *Muse India E-journal* 33 (Sep–Oct 2010).

Bandyopadhyay, Arunendu. *Madhubata Ritayate: Rabindranather Sthapatya o Paribeshbhabna (Collection of Essays on Tagore's Concept of Architecture and Environment)* (Kolkata: Paschimbanga Bangla Akademi, 2005).

Bandyopadhyay, Debarati. 'Tagore, Environment and Ecology: a Place-Space Dynamics.' *Tagore—At Home in the World* ed. Sanjukta Dasgupta and Chinmoy Guha. (New Delhi: Sage, 2013) 305–316.

'Rabindranath Tagore: An Ecocritical Reading' *Towards Tagore* ed. Sanjukta Dasgupta, Ramkumar Mukhopadhyay and Swati Ganguly (Kolkata: Visva-Bharati, 2014) 202–214.

Banerjee, Arunendu. *Rabindranath Tagore and Patrick Geddes: The Ecological Cultural Visionaries* (Kolkata: Asiatic Society, 2005).

Bhaduri, Jnanendralal and Jayanta Kumar Bhaduri. *Rabindrakabye Pranipriti* (Santiniketan: Visva-Bharati Research, 1991).

Bhattacharya, Sabyasachi. Introduction *The Mahatma and the Poet: Letters and Debates between Gandhi and Tagore 1915–1941* ed. Sabyasachi Bhattacharya (New Delhi: National Book Trust, 1997), 1–37.

Bhattacharji, Sukumari. *Literature in the Vedic Age Vol. II The Brahmanas, Aranyakas, Upanishads and Vedanga Sutras* (Calcutta: K.P. Bagchi &

Company, 1986).

Buell, Lawrence. *Writing for an Endangered World: Literature, Culture, and Environment in the U.S. and Beyond* (Cambridge, Massachusetts and London: Belknap-Harvard, 2001).

Das, Sisir Kumar. Introduction. *Rabindranath Tagore: Selected Writings on Literature and Language,* ed. Sisir Kumar Das and Sukanta Chaudhuri (New Delhi: Oxford University Press, 2001) 1–21.

Datta, Nandan. 'Festival of the Earth: Rabindranath Tagore's Environmental Vision.' *California Literary Review* 2007 http://calitreview.com/8 22 July 2011.

Dwivedi, O.P. and B.N. Tiwari, 'Environmental Protection in the Hindu Religion' *Ethical Perspectives on Environmental Issues in India* ed. George A. James (New Delhi: A.P.H. Publishing Corporation, 1999), 161–187.

Egan, Gabriel. 'Shakespeare and Ecocriticism' *Literature Compass,* 12 January 2010.

Elmhirst, Leonard K. *Poet and Plowman* (Kolkata: Visva-Bharati, 2008).

Farr, Cecilia Konchar. 'American Ecobiography,' in *Literature of Nature: An International Sourcebook,* ed. Patrick D. Murphy, Terry Gifford, and Katsunori Yamazato (Chicago and London: Fitzroy Dearborn Publishers, 1998) 94–97.

Garrard, Greg. *Ecocriticism* (London and New York: Routledge, 2004).

Ghosh, Tapobrata. Introduction tr. Sukanta Chaudhuri *Rabindranath Tagore: Selected Short Stories* ed. Sukanta Chaudhuri (New Delhi: Oxford UP, 2000). 1–29.

Glotfelty, Cheryll. 'Literary Studies in an Age of Environmental Crisis' *The Ecocriticism Reader: Landmarks in Literary Ecology* ed. Cheryll Glotfelty and Harold Fromm (Athens and London: University of Georgia Press, 1996) xv–xxxvii.

Fraser, Bashabi. *The Tagore-Geddes Correspondence* (Calcutta: Visva-Bharati, 2004).

Guha, Ramchandra. Introduction, *The Use and Abuse of Nature* Madhav Gadgil and Ramchandra Guha (New Delhi: Oxford University Press, 2000).

Guha, Ranajit. *History at the Limit of World-History* (New York: Columbia

UP, 2002).

Kerridge, Richard. 'Ecological Hardy' in *Beyond Nature Writing: Expanding the Boundaries of Ecocriticism* ed. Karla Armbruster and Kathleen R. Wallace (Charlottesville: University Press of Virginia, 2001) 126–142.

Kripalani, Krishna. *Rabindranath Tagore: A Biography* (1962) (Calcutta: UBSPD in association with Visva-Bharati, 2008).

Tagore: A Life (New Delhi: National Book Trust, 1986).

Lodge, David. *The Art of Fiction* (London: Penguin, 1992).

MacDonald, M.N. 'Indigo planting in India' *Pearson's Magazine* 10(1900): 387–392. 5 April 2014.

Majumdar, Ujjwal. *Visva-bhara Pran: Paribeshbhabuk o Rupakar Rabindranath* (Kolkata: Ebong Mushaira) 2009.

Mies, Maria and Vandana Shiva, *Ecofeminism,* Indian ed. (Jaipur: Rawat, 2010).

Misra, Vidya Niwas. 'Man, Nature and the Poet' *Creativity and Environment* ed. Vidya Niwas Misra (New Delhi: Sahitya Akademi, 1992) 56–61.

Mitra, Dinabandhu. *Nil Darpan, or The Indigo Planter's Mirror* tr. Michael Madhusudan Dutt *Madhusudan Rachanavali* ed. Prafulla Kumar Patra (Calcutta: Patra's, 1986) 668–727.

Neogy, Ajit K. *The Twin Dreams of Rabindranath Tagore: Santiniketan and Sriniketan* (New Delhi: National Book Trust, 2010).

Nixon, Rob. 'Environmentalism and Postcolonialism.' *Postcolonial Studies and Beyond* ed. Ania Loomba et al (New Delhi: Permanent Black, 2006).

Pal, Prasanta Kumar. *Rabijibani,* Volume I (Kolkata: Ananda Publishers, 2012)

Rabijibani Volume II (Kolkata: Ananda, 1990).

Raha, Bipasha. 'Rabindranath Tagore; Attempt at Revival of Villages' *Rabindranath Tagore and the Nation: Essays in Politics, Society and Culture,* ed. Swati Ganguly and Abhijit Sen. (Kolkata: Punascha in association with Visva-Bharati, 2011) 179–190.

The Plough and the Pen: Peasantry, Agriculture and the Literati in Colonial Bengal (New Delhi: Manohar, 2012).

Living a Dream: Rabindranath Tagore and Rural Resuscitation (New Delhi: Manohar, 2014).

Ray, Amit. 'Rabindranath Tagore's Vision of Ecological Harmony' *Ethical Perspectives on Environmental Issues in India* ed. George A. James (New Delhi: A.P.H. Publishing Corporation, 1999) 217–240.

Ray, Mohit K. and Rama Kundu '*Gora*: A Critical Introduction' *Gora* by Rabindranath Tagore tr. Mohit K. Ray and Rama Kundu (New Delhi: Atlantic, 2008) vii–xxvi.

Ray, Mohit Kumar. '*The Ramayana*, *Raktakarabi* and *Surfacing*: An Eco-Feminist Perspective' in *Studies in Literary Criticism* ed. Mohit K. Ray (New Delhi: Atlantic, 2002) 236–242.

Sayre, Robert F. 'Autobiography and the Making of America,' in *Autobiography: Essays Theoretical and Critical*, ed. James Olney (Princeton, New Jersey and Guildford, England: Princeton University Press, 1980) 146–168.

Sen, Sudhir. 'Tagore's Ideas of Social and Economic Development: Realizing them on a Global scale in a revolutionary Age' *Rabindranath Tagore in Perspective: A Bunch of Essays (125th Tagore Birth Anniversary Commemoration Volume)* (Calcutta: Visva-Bharati, 1989) 14–40.

Sen, Sukumar. *History of Bengali Literature* (New Delhi: Sahitya Akademi, 1960) 183.

Sengupta, Kalyan. 'Rabindranath Tagore 1861-1941' *Fifty Key Thinkers on the Environment* ed. Joy A. Palmer (London and New York: Routledge, 2001) 143–146.

Shiva, Vandana. 'Ecology, Equity and Self-reliance' in *The Challenge of South Asia: Development, Democracy and Regional Cooperation* ed. Poorna Wignaraja and Akmal Hussain (Tokyo and New Delhi: United Nations University and Sage, 1989) 75–87.

Spangenberg, B. Review of *The Blue Mutiny: The Indigo Disturbances in Bengal 1859–1862*, by Blair B. Kling in *Modern Asian Studies* 2.2 (1968): 167–169. *JSTOR*. 8 April 2014.

Sukla, A.C. 'Aesthetics as Mass Culture in Indian Antiquity: Rasa, Srngara and Srngara Rasa' in *Dialogue and Universalism* ed. Sonja Servomaa (Warsaw: University of Warsaw, 1997) 91–99.

Tagore, Rabindranath. 'Balai' tr. Palash Baran Pal *Rabindranath Tagore: Selected Short Stories* ed. Sukanta Chaudhuri (New Delhi: Oxford UP, 2000) 255–9.

Boyhood Days tr. Radha Chakravarty (New Delhi: Puffin, 2007).

'The Child's Return' in *Collected Stories* (Delhi: Macmillan, 2001) 46–61.

Chhinnapatravali (Calcutta: Visva-Bharati, 1960).

'Civilization and Progress' in *Rabindranath Tagore: Lectures and Addresses*, ed. Anthony X. Soares (Delhi: Macmillan, 1970) 66–86.

'Cloud and Sun' tr. Indira Devi Chaudhurani in *Boundless Sky: Rabindranath Tagore* (Kolkata: Visva-Bharati, 2006) 22–55.

Chithipatra Vol. V (Kolkata: Visva-Bharati, 1994).

Crisis in Civilization (1941) (Calcutta: Visva-Bharati, 2000).

The English Writings of Rabindranath Tagore Vol. 1 ed. Sisir Kumar Das (New Delhi: Sahitya Akademi, 2001).

The English Writings of Rabindranath Tagore Vol. 2 ed. Sisir Kumar Das (New Delhi: Sahitya Akademi, 2001).

The English Writings of Rabindranath Tagore Vol. 3 ed. Sisir Kumar Das (New Delhi: Sahitya Akademi, 2002).

The English Writings of Rabindranath Tagore Vol. 4 ed. Nitya Priya Ghosh (New Delhi: Sahitya Akademi, 2007).

'From *My Reminiscences*' in *Rabindranath Tagore: An Anthology* ed. Krishna Dutta and Andrew Robinson (London: Picador, 1999) 55–83.

'Glimpses of Bengal by Sir Rabindranath Tagore.' *Fullbooks*. http://www.fullbooks.com/Glimpses-of-Bengal11.html. 28 August 2011.

Gora, tr. Sujit Mukherjee (New Delhi: Sahitya Akademi, 1997).

Gora. Rabindranath Tagore Omnibus 1 (New Delhi: Rupa, 2003) 211–784.

'The Hidden Treasure' *More Stories* (Kolkata: Projapoti, 2009) 118–135.

'Historicality in Literature' tr. Ranajit Guha. *History at the Limit of World-History*. New York: Columbia University Press, 2002) 95–99.

'Ideals of Education,' (1929) *Boundless Sky* (Kolkata: Visva-Bharati, 2006) 285–290.

'Introduction to The Robbery of the Soil' *Poet and Plowman* Leonard K Elmhirst (Kolkata: Visva-Bharati, 2008) 17–25.

Journey to Persia and Iraq: 1932 ed. Supriya Roy (Kolkata: Visva-

Bharati, 2003).

'Hymn to the Tree' tr. Supriya Chaudhuri *Rabindranath Tagore: Selected Poems* ed. Sukanta Chaudhuri (New Delhi: Oxford University Press, 2004) 261–2.

Letter in *The Mahatma and the Poet: Letters and Debates between Gandhi and Tagore 1915–1941* ed. Sabyasachi Bhattacharya (New Delhi: National Book Trust, 1997).

Man (New Delhi: Rupa and Co, 2002).

My Boyhood Days, Rabindranath Tagore Omnibus 1 (New Delhi: Rupa, 2003) 785–852.

My Life in My Words ed. Uma Das Gupta (New Delhi: Penguin Books, 2010).

My Reminiscences (New Delhi: Rupa, 2008).

Poem 67 *Poems* (1942) (Calcutta: Visva-Bharati, 2003).

'The Postmaster' tr. Debendranath Mitter in *Mashi and Other Stories*. (1918) (Delhi: Macmillan, 2001) 161–171.

Preface. *Raktakarabi* tr Mohit K. Ray 'The Ramayana, Raktakarabi and Surfacing: An Eco-Feminist Perspective.'

Studies in Literary Criticism (New Delhi: Atlantic, 2002) 236–242.

'Robbery of the Soil' in *Poet and Plowman* (Kolkata: Visva-Bharati, 2008) 17–25.

'Ryoter Katha' *Kalantar Rabindra Rachanavali* Vol. 12 (Kolkata: Visva-Bharati, 1989) 651–657.

'Shakuntala' tr. Sukanta Chaudhuri *Rabindranath Tagore: Selected Writings on Literature and Language* ed. Sisir Kumar Das and Sukanta Chaudhuri (New Delhi: Oxford University Press, 2001) 237–251.

'Subha' tr. Supriya Chaudhuri *Rabindranath Tagore: Selected Short Stories* ed. Sukanta Chaudhuri (New Delhi: Oxford University Press, 2000)104–109.

'Trespass' tr. Meenakshi Mukherjee *Rabindranath Tagore: Selected Short Stories* ed. Sukanta Chaudhuri (New Delhi: Oxford University Press, 2000)121–125.

Tagore, Rathindranath. *On the Edges of Time* (1958) (Kolkata: Visva-Bharati, 1981)